4.95

C000144337

The Rebirth and Restoration of Israel

Murray Dixon

Sovereign World

Sovereign World
P.O. Box 17
Chichester PO20 6RY
England

Printed and bound in Great Britain by
Anchor Brendon Ltd, Tiptree, Essex

ISBN 1 85240 012 9

Contents

Acknowledgements

The material for this book has built up over a period of at least seven years during which time I have avidly read and listened to teaching concerning Jewish-Christian relations and the inheritance God has prepared for both these His covenant peoples. My thinking has, therefore, been influenced by many people whom I am unable to name but I particularly want to acknowledge my heart-felt gratitude to Dr Derek Prince, Mr Lance Lambert and the Reverend David Pawson who provided an oasis at a time when I was very thirsty.

During my first visit to Israel, a Jewess who confessed Yeshua as Messiah challenged me: 'If you Christians don't pray for the Jews, who will?' Not only have I never been able to forget her heart-cry but I was also reminded of Jesus' words: *'From the one who has been entrusted with much, much more will be asked'* (*Luke 12*:48). I owe much to this daughter of Zion who ensured I was involved in Israel's restoration.

My understanding has developed as I have listened to Jewish people during my several subsequent visits to Israel, and as I have questioned them. The questions posed to me by pilgrims in the various groups we have led to Israel and members of the many congregations with whom I have been privileged to speak have stimulated deeper thinking and research, while the various opportunities of living with Israeli families has deepened my awareness of how little I have learned and understood. To all these people I am indebted.

I am extremely thankful to Ken Burnett for his friendship, his encouragement, and for his patience and wisdom as he read through my script making those needful suggestions for correction and improvement. Alison Bartlett's proof reading and suggestions have sharpened the text and my family who have borne inconvenience are rewarded with the fulfilment I have received in pursuing this burning concern within me.

5

Dedication

To Rosemary, my encouraging wife; Rowan, Jeremy and Ruth, my family who share the burden; and to the host of unknown intercessors for Israel.

Foreword

While the crucifixion and death of Jesus, King of the Jews, occurred (by the permission and foreknowledge of God) at the hands of Jews and Gentiles – misguided and sinful representatives of the whole human race, including you and me – His glorious resurrection was at the hands of none less than God, the Father – El Shaddai, God Almighty. Of course, most born-again Christians know this.

What is less realised, or perhaps completely unrealised, is that there are many solemn parallels between that brief earthly history of the King of the Jews, and the subsequent history of the Jews themselves.

Misguided zealots, including many leading Churchmen, have shouted down through the ages to this very century: 'DEATH TO THE JEWS!' and they have lost no time in acting to bring that curse and threat to fulfilment. History proves it, as the pages of this book so harrowingly outline. Christians who do not know how to blush, who do not know how to feel ashamed of Church history, who do not know that salvation was (and IS) of the Jews, who do not have a tear in their hearts for the Jewish nation, would read this book with advantage.

For others, especially those who realise that the death of Jesus was ordained according to the foreknowledge of God (*Acts* 2:23, *Isaiah* 53:10), the pages of this book will help to seal the conviction of an indebtedness to the Jewish race – not only for the revelation of God brought to the world by and through them, but also for the awful sufferings of the Lord Himself. There are nonetheless, tragic, but clear parallels in the history of Israel and its people.

To the fact that, as a nation, and also as millions of individuals, the Jewish people have died a death at the hands of cruel and vindictive men – the pages of world history bear an only too-horrifying witness. No other people have been so evicted from country after country, so constantly pillaged of possessions, so burnt alive, so endured the most sophisticated national plots against them for their mass and total extermination! No other people have been so oppressed by the laws of 'civilised countries' as to be allowed only particular and disreputable forms of employment! No other nation has, in fact, been made a scapegoat, and such a scapegoat, for the sins of others.

But therein lies the parallel – the Messianic parallel! Although by no means without severe guilt – quite obviously the only nation prepared to bring the Messiah bears a greater responsibility in Messianic rejection than other nations – it is nonetheless important to realise that the Jewish nation did act, has acted, and continues to act as a scapegoat for the outpoured judgment of God. One dictionary description of the term 'scapegoat' is: 'anyone who has to shoulder the blame due to another.'

While it is generally agreed that Jesus died for the sins of the world, that 'He was bruised for our transgressions,' it is seldom acknowledged that 'we' (the Gentile world) ALSO hid our faces from Him and that the crucifixion was a universal sin. However, the focal point of the New Testament theology, the Letter to the Romans, makes it quite clear in a short pithy statement (that is never expounded or preached upon!) that *'concerning the Gospel, they (Israel) are enemies FOR YOUR SAKE (the Gentiles)'* (*Romans 11*:28).

In other words, Jewish national reaction to, and rejection of Jesus has resulted in benefit to the Gentiles. What an incredible statement: 'for YOUR sake!' What on earth is God meaning here? The same chapter gives us at least three answers:

(1) The main part of the nation (but not all) have been cut off, temporarily laid aside, from a relationship with God – sent 'into the wilderness' like the scapegoat (*Ezekiel 20*:35). Gentile nations have escaped this (*Romans 11*:17).

(2) God has given them a spirit of stupor, which is unlike that on other nations (*Romans 11*:8).

(3) As a direct result of their fall from grace, salvation has come to the Gentiles. Hypothetically, therefore, had Israel accepted the Messiah, *no* salvation would have come to the Gentiles! (*Romans 11*:11).

Obviously, then, this is what the Holy Spirit is endeavouring to teach us when Holy Writ says to us, 'They (the Jewish nation) are enemies of the gospel for your (the Gentiles') sake.' Had

8

Christendom earlier, had evil men earlier, had zealous Christians earlier seen this truth – there is the deepest indebtedness to the Jewish people over their enduring the brunt of God's judgment on behalf of the rest of the world – what changes would history have not seen? What murders and massacres would have been removed from the middle ages and the current age? What provoking of the Jews to jealousy to know their own God of Israel personally might have replaced our provoking of them to further hardness against the One, the Messiah, we claim to stand for and to represent?

Murray Dixon's excellent book tabulates much of that of which we need to repent. It is a book which ought to be in the hands of ANYONE who wants to be aware of God's priorities today, because, the book does not just *end* on the wilderness experience, the crucifixion of the Jewish nation. The most-often repeated promise in the Bible, the restoration of Israel, gains apt attention and teaching – and you will be enabled not only to thank God for His faithfulness and mercy, and for what He is doing today – but you will also be enabled to take up the prayer burden for God's people who ARE STILL 'beloved for the sake of the fathers', the patriarchs. Whatever you do – do not miss the latter calling as you come to the end of these anointed pages. The spiritual resurrection of the Jewish nation will astonish the world! (*Isaiah 60*:1–3)

What about the author himself – Murray? I know him as a man of high integrity, a true servant of the Living God who desires also to serve his brethren. Seasoned as a Chaplain for many years to members of the New Zealand Air Force, God has been leading him into a ministry of prayer for the Restoration in every sense of the word, of God's earthly people – Israel. You can be confident that Murray always keeps the Lord first before his eyes, and that he has on his heart the fuller manifestation of God's glory to this world through the revelation of the Messiah to the entire Jewish race.

As you read, may the Lord's blessing be upon you.

Ken Burnett
Director,
Prayer for Israel

Estimates of Jewish Victims During the Holocaust

Polish-Soviet area	4,565,000
Germany	125,000
Austria	65,000
Czechoslovakia (in the pre-Munich boundaries)	277,000
Hungary, including northern Transylvania	402,000
France	83,000
Belgium	24,000
Luxembourg	700
Italy	7,500
The Netherlands	106,000
Norway	760
Rumania (Regat, southern Transylvania, southern Bukovina)	40,000
Yugoslavia	60,000
Greece	65,000
TOTAL LOSS	5,820,960

Preface

My reading of Jewish history during the Church period has resulted in considerable inner anguish and even weeping as I have discovered the depths of inhuman treatment vented upon this ancient people. Accompanying this sense of anguish is my shame for the horrific treatment we Christians have been guilty of perpetrating in the lives of Jewish people for generations and the wider ramifications this influence has exerted.

So deeply entrenched is antisemitism that we use many phrases, terms of reference and jokes destructive to Jewish people, and they are often used unwittingly, but nevertheless find their roots in antisemitism. We often hear a hard-hearted money lender or unscrupulous businessman referred to as a 'Shylock'. A reminder of Shakespeare's immortalised caricature of the Jew as a monstrous bloodthirsty usurer.

How frequently do we participate in a rousing cheer: 'Hip! Hip! Hooray!'? Originally 'Hep! Hep!' – (a derogatory rallying cry against the Jewish people), it is said to have been the Crusaders rallying cry and certainly used in the anti-Jewish riots of Germany. The term derives from the initials of 'Hierosolyma est perdita' – 'Jerusalem is lost!' which was the rejoicing cry of many in Greece at the misfortunes of Jerusalem in the 1st century.

Even our censuring judgment on some form of action which we describe as 'beyond the Pale', originates from the unjust confinement of Jews in settlement in Poland. I have often heard preachers refer to the Israelites in order to illustrate blindness and hardness of heart but rarely refer to their examples of faithfulness and obedience. And so, I could continue, but the point is made.

It has been a shocking awakening to me, as I suspect it will be to many Christians, to realise the extent of unbiblical teaching concerning the Jewish people within the Church. The resulting wicked behaviour ensuing from that teaching – climaxing in the infamous attempt to destroy all the Jews in the Holocaust – has been something even harder, perhaps impossible for me to fully

11

grasp. Therein, surmounting the centuries of erroneous teaching, we have seen the Crucifixion of the Jews, from which by God's overruling we have also witnessed their physical Resurrection.

I have endeavoured to trace the roots and development of this erroneous teaching in the hope that its exposure will lead to a better understanding of the truth.

We need to understand the Church's Jewish roots, the place God has determined for Israel in history, the relationship of the Church with Israel and the responsibility of the Church to Israel if we are going to make sense of history and understand the complete function of the Church. I have begun this book by demonstrating the Jewishness of Jesus and the significance of His Jewishness.

Following some observations on the revelation Paul received of the mystery of the Church, I have examined his teaching to a dividing Church, noticing the inheritances promised to Israel and the Church. Within the ensuing three centuries, the Church leaders separated the Church from the Jews and the Bible from its Jewishness. The extent of this error is witnessed in the record of the compounding tragedies suffered by both the Jewish people and the Church in the centuries which followed.

During the Evangelical revival of the 19th century, the return to the Bible stimulated a change of heart towards the Jewish people. Not only was there expression of concern for the restoration of the Jewish homeland but there emerged a genuine concern for the Jewish people. Many Jewish people were touched by this authentic concern for them, and this led to recognition by a goodly number of Jesus as their Redeemer. Coinciding with this turning point, emerged the Zionist movement and plans for the restoration of their ancient homeland. As the 20th century has progressed, the fulfilment of the promises to both Israel and the Church have been evident, the parallel Church restoration laying in the renewed work of the Holy Spirit.

Before us lies the challenge to make up for the years of inexpressible but repairable damage that we Christians have been responsible for to the Jewish people. We do need to understand the past in order to act in accordance with God's will and purpose for the future. It is my prayer that you will be challenged into action as I myself have felt the need to be.

Murray Dixon   1987
Rosh Hashana

1

'The Truth Will Set You Free'

(*John* 8:32)

'Forgive us for crucifying Thee a second time in their flesh. For, O Lord, we know not what we did.'

These words conclude a prayer of repentance uttered by Pope John XXIII, for actions by Christians towards the Jewish people. A prayer which needs to flow from the hearts of Christians worldwide.

Not until we are familiar with the Church's behaviour for nineteen hundred years towards the Jewish people do we understand the deep significance of this prayer. Nor do we realise, until we have opened the history books, how deeply seated is the antisemitic teaching in the church that even today influences Biblical interpretation and Christian action. The Church has been so involved in accusing the Jews of 'deicide' – the killing of God – that we Christians stand accountable to the charge of 'genocide'.

The horrific facts of the Nazi Holocaust in Second World War Europe mark the end of a period of history. Not only does **the Holocaust** represent a calculated attempt at the genocide of the Jewish people but it also **marks the lowest ebb of man's inhumanity to man sanctioned by the Church by her interlude of silence**.

A Jewish theologian, Dr Jakob Jocz, made an astute observation in his book 'The Jewish People and Jesus Christ After Auschwitz',

'Auschwitz is a landmark ranking high in the scale of tragic events in the history of the Jewish people, equal to, if not surpassing, the tragedy of the Fall of Jerusalem in A.D. 70. Auschwitz is not only a tragedy for Jews; it is a tragedy for mankind.

'After Auschwitz' marks the possibility of a new beginning for the Jewish people, for the Church, for the world. In regard to Jewish-Christian relationships two events are of

13

outstanding importance: the creation of the State of Israel and Vatican II. Both these events will have far-reaching consequences for the future.'[1]

Second thoughts

Declarations from the Roman Catholic Church's Vatican Council of 1962–1965 – the legislative body of the Church – not only reflect a careful analysis of both scripture and Church history regarding the Jewish people, but also make statements reversing their entire theological perception.*

The traumatic event of the Holocaust and the startling event of the rebirth of Israel have caused many Christian teachers to rethink the Biblical exegesis which claims that God has concluded His dealings with Israel and the Jewish people and now the Church can exclusively claim their promises as her own. The rebirth of Israel within her promised borders on May 14, 1948, and the fact that her multitudinous neighbours and enemies have not succeeded in destroying Israel in her 40 years existence, have caused some within the Church to rethink their own position.

Repentance means a change of heart

John Stott, the evangelical theologian says,

'We need to get the failures of the Church on our conscience, to feel the offence to Christ and the world which these failures are, to weep over the credibility gap between the Church's talk and the Church's walk, to repent of our readiness to excuse and even condone our failures, and to determine to do something about it.'[2]

Nowhere is this more applicable than in our history and relationship with the Jewish people. Evidence worldwide reflects a characteristic change of heart among many Christians, sometimes sentimental, while with others very practical, but nevertheless repentant.

Discovery of our Jewish roots as Christians is persuading gentile Christians to re-read the Bible with new understanding,

---

* The statement is found in appendix 1.

14

recognising the Jewish emphasis. As increasing numbers of Jewish people are finding the fulfilment of their faith in the New Testament, they are providing the Church with a new dimension of teaching and understanding that not only brings Christians and Jews together, but shatters long-standing prejudices and provides the Church with a fresh vision.

In our reading of scripture we have often failed to recognise the identity of both the writer and those for whom it was meant primarily. We have been guilty of appropriating what suits us without due respect to whom the promises, statements, commandments, blessings and curses were addressed. We even have evidence of alterations by translators to suit their own purposes.**

Restored truth

As Israel is being restored, archaeological discoveries are upholding the authenticity of Scripture refuting the confusion raised by modernists – the discovery of the Dead Sea Scrolls at Qumran in 1947 being the major find to date. Some teachers stated that Isaiah chapters 52 and 53, prophesying the details of Jesus' death, were altered after His death to correct the scriptural record thus undermining the prophetic aspect of the word. Since the texts formerly used by our translators only date back to the sixth century A.D. the argument could not be disproved. However, with the Qumran discovery we now have a text of Isaiah dating back to 100 years before Jesus' crucifixion and this text corresponds with the later texts, thereby proving the authority of the prophetic writing.

The restoration of the Hebrew language, which had not been used as an everyday language since the final dispersion of the Jewish people from their land in the second century, has provided a key to Biblical understanding. Some eminent biblical scholars working in Israel are convinced that the first language of the New Testament was Hebrew – not Aramaic as has long been held.

** An example of mistranslation is evidenced in the version authorised by King James I, published in England in 1611. In the New Testament an extraordinary exchange was made. Wherever the name 'Jacob' occurred it was replaced by the King's name, 'James'. 'James' is not a Jewish name, it appears nowhere in the Old Testament and there is no mention in the New Testament of the common Jewish name 'Jacob', (other than through quotations from the old Testament).

Dr Robert Lindsey described his discovery, when translating the gospel of Mark into Hebrew, of a strong Hebraism in the gospels of Matthew, Mark and Luke. His attention was caught by the very Hebraic word order of the Greek text of Mark.

Dr David Bivin and Dr Roy Blizzard, in their book, 'Understanding the Difficult Words of Jesus', explain that our modern translations of the New Testament are translated from a Greek text that derives from an earlier Greek text, originally taken from a Hebrew 'Life of Jesus'. The writings of the early Church Fathers refer to the gospels in Hebrew although no such evidence has yet been unearthed. From their studies they deduce that 91% of the original entire Bible was written in Hebrew.

The root of the problem lies in trying to translate Hebrew words and idioms into Greek which became meaningless and even more mystifying when translated into English. An example is the unusual word 'ochloi' that occurs frequently in the gospels and has been translated 'multitudes' which does not fit the text. It has been discovered that the rabbis used the word 'ochloism' which is plural for 'the people of the locality'. Not only does this meaning satisfy the context but it clarifies the meaning. Although no Hebrew text has yet been discovered these scholars have demonstrated that difficult scriptural phrases translated from the Greek, which have puzzled Bible scholars for generations, are given clear meaning when translated back into Hebrew.

Bivin and Blizzard state,

'Many scholars in Israel are now convinced that the spoken and written language of the Jews in the Land of Israel at the time of Jesus was indeed Hebrew; and that the Synoptic Gospels were derived from original Hebrew sources.'[3]

William Albright, the expert archaeologist on the ancient Middle East, supports these claims. After the discovery of the Dead Sea Scrolls, he spoke of the Jewishness of the Bible not only being confirmed but being, in fact, more Jewish than previously thought. 'It was written entirely by Jews, with a spiritual and literary background in the Bible and the proto-rabbinic culture. So it remains a Jewish work . . .' Albright emphasised the importance of the Dead Sea discovery concluding 'it becomes more Jewish than we had thought – as truly Jewish as the Old Testament is Israelite.'[4]

16

The Psalmist spoke prophetically,

'But you, O Lord, sit enthroned forever; your renown endures through all generations. You will arise and have compassion on Zion, for it is time to show favour to her; the appointed time has come.'[5]

Dr Derek Prince, while explaining that today God is restoring both Israel and the Church, comments on these verses from Psalm 102 and their association with *Acts 3*:20–21, noting the distinction between Israel and the Church:

'Here we have a clear reference to the same period and the same purposes of God. When we read 'Zion' in the Bible I think we should understand it in part at least, as the assembly of God's people. As I understand it 'Zion' is a word that is used for all who are related to God as His people by a covenant. It is really the one word that covers Israel and the Church. **I do not believe the Church is ever called Israel or that Israel is ever called the Church, but this word 'Zion' does cover both God's people: the natural people, Israel, and the spiritual people, the Church . . .**

So, in the New Testament and the Old alike, we have this clear prediction of a time of restoration, a time of rebuilding when God is going to intervene in sovereign grace and in mercy on behalf of his people, to restore them and to build them up. This is the period when we may confidently look for the return of the Lord Jesus Christ, his appearance in glory.'[6]

The restoration of Zion – the Church and Israel – is not only a parallel restoration but a restoration where each are dependent upon the other. God's eternal purpose expressed in the prophets to restore His people to the Land, and the Land to His people, seems to have largely been ignored by both the Jews and the Church. It has taken overwhelming tragedy to achieve this plan and to cause the Church to take another look at the Scriptures in order to understand what God is doing in our time. As the Church begins to perceive how her destiny and that of Israel are interwoven, she will earnestly desire to respond to what the Holy Spirit is saying to the Church. *Isaiah 42*:19 is the voice of the Spirit to both Israel and the Church,

'Who is blind but my servant, and deaf like the messenger I send? Who is blind like the one committed to me, blind like the servant of the Lord?'

The Fig Tree and the Vine

Whether we Christians look backwards or forwards we should see our inseparable relationship with Israel. Our Jewish past is reflected in our treasured scriptures written by Jewish hands concerning a Jewish Messiah, Jewish apostles, Jewish prophets, and Jewish patriarchs all in the Jewish language.

But the Jewish contribution does not stop at the close of the Biblical period. Although our surviving records of the Church's history reflect large gaps, they do bear rich testimony to the Jewish contribution. In the words of one writer: 'Limitations of space prevent the inclusion of many Jewish Christians† who have worthily contributed to the growth and glory of the Church . . . Suffice is to say that Hebrew Christians are legion, and are to be found in all walks of life.'[7]

Although not always recognised, Jewish Christians made significant contributions to the Reformation and to the Evangelical Revival of the 19th century. Both Martin Luther and John Wycliffe were profoundly influenced by the 14th century noted biblical scholar and writer, Nicholas of Lyra.[8] Emmanuel Tremellius made an important contribution to the Reformation as a theologian and an outstanding expert on the Hebrew language. He was looked upon as one of the most learned scholars in oriental languages of his time and celebrated for his Latin translation of the Bible. Tremellius was invited to England by Thomas Cranmer to help frame the Thirty-Nine Articles and the compilation of the Book of Common Prayer. It is not widely

---

† JEWISH CHRISTIAN – (a modern current term) is used in this book to denote a Jewish person who has recognised and received the Lord Jesus as Saviour and Lord. Many other terms are sometimes used such as Hebrew Christian, Messianic Jew, completed Jew, fulfilled Jew.

In Jewish circles, *whatever* term is used, the Jew who has declared such a personal faith in Jesus is usually regarded as a 'convert' to Christianity, who has forsaken his Jewishness and 'gone over to the other side', to the Gentile faith. He is often regarded as a traitor.

This is the complete opposite of Scriptural teaching because:

(a) The problem of 'who is a Jew?' is only solved through the work of the Holy Spirit as outlined in *Romans 2*:28–29.

(b) It is the Gentiles who have been converted, and grafted into the Jewish faith (*Ephesians 2*:12–13).

It is Biblically correct to both call and to regard Jewish believers just as 'Jews', Paul said 'I am a Jew', 'I was a Jew'. (*Acts 21*:39 and 22:3).

18

understood that a Jew played such a significant role in the doctrinal and liturgical constitution of the Church of England[9]. Jewish Christian Bible translators, theologians, writers and historians countered the destructive inroads of rationalism into the 19th century European Church.‡

Our promised future, described in both the Old Testament and the New, tells of an awesome revival in Israel as the Holy Spirit brings alive the faith of the Jewish people to reveal the glory of the God of Israel to the non-Jewish world:

> '*For if their rejection is the reconciliation of the world, what will their acceptance be but life from the dead?*'[10]

We look to a future when the long-awaited Jewish King will rule the earth from Jerusalem whose gates are to be inscribed with the names of the twelves tribes of Israel and the foundations of whose walls are to be inscribed with the names of the twelve Jewish apostles – and there all the nations shall gather.[11]

As the Bible frequently links the fig tree and the vine, the symbols of Israel and the Church, so our destinies are intertwined. While neither can bear the fruit of the other, both are promised fruitfulness – fruit that is now coming to maturity,

> '*The trees are bearing their fruit; the fig tree and the vine yield their riches. Be glad, O people of Zion, rejoice in the Lord your God, for He has given you a teacher for righteousness.*'[12]

Notes

1. Jocz J., *The Jewish People and Jesus Christ After Auschwitz*, p.7–8.
2. Stott J., *God's New Society*.
3. Bivin D. & Blizzard R., *The Difficult Words of Jesus*, p.38.
4. as quoted in *May Your Name be Inscribed in the Book of Life*, p.iii.
5. *Psalm 102*:12–13.
6. Prince D., *Israel and the Church: Parallel Restoration* an address.
7. Gartenhaus, J., *Famous Hebrew Christians*, p.26.
8. ibid, p.26 footnote.
9. Jocz, J., *The Jewish People and Jesus Christ*, p.247.
10. *Romans 11*:15.
11. *Revelation 21*, *Jeremiah 3*:17, *Zechariah 14*:16.
12. *Joel 2*:22–23.

‡ Details of these contributions are reported in chapter 10.

Recommended reading

1. *The Jewish People and Jesus Christ after Auschwitz*, J Jocz.
2. *The Difficult Words of Jesus*, David Bivin and Roy Blizzard.
3. *The Jewish Background to the Lord's Prayer*, Brad Young.

2

The Jewishness of Jesus

'I've been a Christian for over thirty years and I've never realised the importance of Jesus being a Jew. Of course I've always known He is Jewish but I didn't know its significance.'

This was the statement of a man after seeing the gospels in a new light. His comment pinpoints a blindness in the Church concerning God's purposes for Israel and the Jewish people. Let us research the history of the Church and note her attitude towards the Jewish people. Consider Jesus the Jew.

Born To Be King

A Jewish man once said to me, 'I struggled and struggled with the idea that Jesus is the Messiah. I had heard of Jesus and I thought He was for the Catholics, but I am Jewish, so I was convinced He was not for me. One day I read in the New Testament the book by Matthew. I discovered that Jesus is Jewish! Jesus is totally Jewish! He did all the things that a Jew does.'

Matthew opens His gospel with Jesus' genealogy. He begins with Abraham, showing the line through King David. We see that Jesus is not only Jewish but that He is also of royal descent. Luke likewise shows that Jesus is of the royal line. In chapter 2, where he describes Jesus' birth at the time of the census, Mary and Joseph have to travel from Galilee to Bethlehem, 'David's town . . . because Joseph belonged to the house and line of David.'[1] Jesus' royal birth was also acclaimed by non-Jews. Magi had travelled from the distant east to Jerusalem asking the question, 'Where is the One who has been born king of the Jews?'[2] At His crucifixion a sign was placed over His head declaring in Hebrew, Latin and Greek 'This is Jesus, the King of the Jews'. Ensuring that everybody from all nations would know that Jesus is King, this was written in the three common languages of the time. It is not just that Jesus is King. **Jesus is the Jewish King**.

Each gospel writer makes it very plain that Jesus totally participated in Jewish life and faith.

'On the eighth day, when it was time to circumcise him, he was named Jesus, the name the angel had given him before he had been conceived.'[3]

Luke explains from the books of the Law, (see *Leviticus 12*:3), that God ordered this consecration to the Lord of a first-born male. This had been practised by the Jewish people ever since the command was given through Moses and this is exactly what the scripture records,[4]

*'the parents brought in the child Jesus to do for him what the custom of **the Law required**.'*[5]

This is known as Jesus' 'brit mila', or 'covenant of cutting' which every Jewish boy experienced. To be sure that we realise that everything Jewish had been completed before leaving Jerusalem, Luke adds,

*'When Joseph and Mary **had done everything required by the Law** of the Lord, they returned to Galilee . . .'*[6]

The only other detailed event we know about Jesus' childhood is His visit to Jerusalem which Luke deliberately states was at the age of 12 years, although Luke explains that Jesus' parents participated in Passover each year in Jerusalem – presumably with Jesus.

'Every year his parents went to Jerusalem for the Feast of Passover. When he was twelve years old, they went up to the Feast, according to the custom. After the Feast was over, while his parents were returning home, the boy Jesus stayed behind in Jerusalem, but they were unaware of it . . . they found him in the temple courts, sitting among the teachers, listening to them and asking them questions. Everyone who heard him was amazed at his understanding and his answers. When his parents saw him, they were astonished.'[7]

Why has Luke carefully inserted this event making note of Jesus' age? The Jewish scholar Dr Pinchas Lapide believes that during this Passover visit to Jerusalem Jesus underwent His bar-mitzvah.[8] The time when a young Jewish man 'attains religious and legal maturity', when he commits himself to the responsibilities of a member of the community of faith. Jesus' subsequent ability to engage the Jewish elders and doctors of the Law in discussion to the astonishment of others, including Joseph and Mary, not only indicates this to be an important occasion in Jesus' life but again emphasises Jesus' Jewishness.

Lapide makes the following summary:

'Jesus' parents were devout Jews who probably had a mezuzah (a roll of parchment containing some Hebrew scriptures known as the "Shema") on the doorpost of their modest home in Nazareth and kept a kosher kitchen. Aron (the Jewish author, Robert Aron) believes that Mary probably put tzitzit, or fringes, on the child's coat in obedience to an injunction in Deuteronomy 22:12, and that Joseph taught him the carpenter's trade. "Just as it is necessary to feed one's son," says the Talmud, "so it is necessary to teach him a manual trade." Jesus' parents undoubtedly brought him up to recite the benedictions and prayers prescribed for certain hours of the Hebrew day, and sent him to the synagogue for the study of Hebrew and the Law. Perhaps it was at the family's Passover Seder, when an empty chair is placed at the table in case the Prophet Elijah should return, that Jesus first learned about the Messiah. Much of the Lord's prayer paraphrases the old Aramaic prayer, the Kaddish, which Jesus must have learned and absorbed as a youth. Even the beatitudes in the Sermon on the Mount are a direct reflection of common Jewish beliefs that Jesus could have heard from the rabbis at the Nazareth synagogue. . .

What emerges from the gospel accounts, therefore, is the figure of a humble Jewish carpenter, born, circumcised and reared as a Jew, who spent all his earthly life amongst Jews of what today would be called "the lower classes", living and preaching ethical precepts which were imbued with the Torah of Moses and the teachings of Israel's prophets'[8]

As His Custom Was

Years later, after His baptism and His victory over the devil in the wilderness Jesus travelled north,

'*He went to Nazareth, where he had been brought up, and on the Sabbath day he went into the synagogue, as was his custom. And he stood up to read.*'[9]

We are told it was usual for Jesus to attend the synagogue in Nazareth. As with all Jewish boys He had been taken along to synagogue every Sabbath by Joseph and the other sons of the family since His infancy. This was the Jewish practice. However, on this particular occasion He did something very significant. He came forward and read from the scrolls. Jesus had the right to do this only because He had undertaken the responsibility of entering the community of the faithful, otherwise He would not have been permitted that privilege. Jesus is totally Jewish.

If Any Man Thirst

Jesus travelled to Jerusalem to celebrate the Feast of Succot, or Tabernacles, as described in John chapter 7. This feast is prescribed in *Leviticus* chapter 23 verses 33 to 43. It is a thanksgiving at the conclusion of the fruit and vegetable harvest and it is a time to pray for rain in readiness for the planting of the next crops. It has not rained since Passover, six months earlier; the ground is extremely dry after the hot summer and now very warm autumn.

Rain in season in the Middle East is always regarded as a sign of blessing. When rain comes, the people dance for joy! An eighth day is added after the last day of this celebration, which the scripture describes as 'the last and greatest day of the Feast'. The priests carried gold jugs of water up to the altar in the Temple and while the prayers for rain ascended the priests poured the water upon the altar until it spilled down the steps. While this was happening Jesus stood up and said,

> '*If a man is thirsty, let him come to me and drink. Whoever believes in me, as the Scripture has said, streams of living water will flow from within him.*'[10]

About two months after this occasion we see Jesus again travelling to Jerusalem. It is now winter, the month of December. He has come to celebrate the feast of Dedication as recorded in *John* 10:22. This feast, unlike Passover and Tabernacles, is not prescribed by the Law. It is a celebration by the Jewish people of the Dedication of the Temple. It had been instituted by Judas Maccabaeus in 164 B.C. when the Temple which had been desecrated by Antiochus Epiphanes, was cleansed and re-dedicated to the service of God.

When the Temple services were restored by Judas Maccabaeus, the oil was found to have been desecrated. Only one phial of pure oil was discovered. The supply was sufficient to feed the large seven-branch candlestick for one day only. By a miracle the phial lasted for eight days, till a fresh supply could be obtained. In memory of this, it was ordered the following year, that the Temple be illuminated for eight days on the anniversary of its 'Dedication'. This feast, which the Jews still celebrate, is called 'Hanukka'.

The Hem of His Garment

Luke records an event, the significance of which even some Bible translators miss, concerning the action of the woman who had suffered from haemorrhaging for twelve years,

> 'she came up behind Him and **touched the tassel of His garment**; and immediately her flow of blood ceased.'[11]

Jesus was wearing clothing as prescribed by the Law,

> 'Throughout the generations to come you are to make tassels on the corners of your garments, with a blue cord on each tassel. You will have these **tassels** to look at and so you will remember all the commands of the Lord . . .'[12]

The woman seeking healing reached through the crowd to touch the tassels or 'tzitzit' as they are known in Hebrew. At present the tzitzit are worn as a special under-garment or on the prayer shawl, or 'tallith' in Hebrew, but in ancient time they seem to have been worn on the outer garment itself. When this desperate woman thrust her hand through the crowd towards Jesus she deliberately reached to grasp the tzitzit knowing the touch of God could heal her instantly.

Jesus The Messiah in the Jewish Scriptures

Jesus' Jewishness is even further demonstrated as we read the Jewish Scriptures. As far back as Eden God foretold His plan of redemption through the promised Messiah:

> 'I will put enmity between you (Satan) and the woman (Mary – who mothered Jesus), and between your seed and her seed; he shall bruise your head, and you shall bruise his heel.'[13]

25

Jacob, the Jewish patriarch, prophesied of the promised Messiah's victory as a king returning from battle, ruling the nations:

> *'You are a lion's cub, O Judah; you return from the prey, my son . . . the sceptre will not depart from Judah, nor the ruler's staff from between his feet, until he comes to whom it belongs, and the obedience of the nations is his.'*[14]

Israel's God explains that the only way of atonement is by shedding blood:

> *'For the life of a creature is in the blood, and I have given it to you to make atonement for yourselves on the altar; it is* ***the blood that makes atonement for one's life.'***[15]

Moses speaks of his own ministry as being a foreshadowing of Messiah's ministry, adding that Messiah will be Jewish – and describes Him as a 'brother':

> *'The Lord your God will raise up for you a prophet like me from among* ***your own brothers.*** *You must listen to him.'*[16]

Centuries later God began to reveal details of Messiah – who He would be, where He would come from, what He would accomplish, how He would accomplish His work.

Following on from *Genesis 3*:15 we are now told the 'seed' would come through a Jewish woman and that the birth would be a 'sign'. Just as the unusual nature of Isaac's birth had been a sign to Abraham of God's keeping His covenant in bringing to birth the Jewish nation, so the unique nature of this 'virgin' birth would be a sign to the Jewish people. Contained in this child's name is the revelation of a mystery – Immanuel – God with us. In the Messiah of Israel God would be present.

> *'Therefore the Lord himself will give you a sign: The virgin will be with child and will give birth to a son, and will call him Immanuel.'*[17]

Jacob had revealed that Messiah would rule over the nations. Isaiah prophesied that He would rule eternally from the Jewish throne of David in peace and justice:

> *'For to us a child is born, to us a Son is given, and the government will be on His shoulders. And He will be called Wonderful Counsellor, Mighty God, Everlasting Father, Prince of Peace.*

*Of the increase of His government and peace there will be no end.
He will reign on David's throne and over His kingdom, establishing and upholding it with justice and righteousness from that time
on and for ever.'*[18]

Micah, the Jewish prophet, predicted the birth-place of Israel's eternal Ruler:

*'But you, Bethlehem Ephrathah, though you are small among the
clans of Judah, out of you will come for me one who will be Ruler
over Israel, whose origins are from of old, from ancient times.'*[19]

That Messiah would come through the House of David is confirmed – He would be of the stock of Jesse, David's father. A detailed description of the nature of Messiah's rule and life during that reign is revealed in verse 2 to 10 of Isaiah 11:

*'A shoot will come up from the stump of Jesse; from his roots a
Branch will bear fruit . . .'*[20]

With great emphasis, Isaiah focuses upon the atoning work of the Messiah as the seed of the woman. **He will make atonement with His own blood, becoming the sacrifice Himself. It is God's will that Messiah is the sacrifice.** We need to notice that the phrase **'my people' refers to the Jewish people**.

*'He grew up before him like a tender shoot, and like a root out of
dry ground.
He had no beauty or majesty to attract us to him, nothing in his
appearance that we should desire him.
He was despised and rejected by men, a man of sorrows, and
familiar with suffering . . .
Surely he took up our infirmities and carried our sorrows, yet we
considered him stricken by God, smitten by Him, and afflicted.
But he was pierced for our transgressions, he was crushed for our
iniquities; the punishment that brought us peace was upon him,
and by his wounds we are healed . . .
For he was cut off from the land of the living; for the transgression
of **my people** he was stricken.
He was assigned a grave with the wicked, and with the rich in his
death, though he had done no violence, nor was any deceit in his
mouth.
Yet it was the Lord's will to crush him and cause him to suffer,
and though the Lord makes his life a guilt offering, he will see his*

offspring and prolong his days, and the will of the Lord will
prosper in his hand . . .
For he bore the sin of many, and made intercession for the
transgressors.'[21]

In contrast to this description of the Messiah's suffering seen
from the observer's viewpoint, David is given insight into Messiah's suffering from Messiah's viewpoint:

'My God, my God, why have you forsaken me? Why are you so
far from saving me? . . . All who see me mock me; they hurl
insults, shaking their heads: 'He trusts in the Lord; let the Lord
rescue him'. . . Many bulls surround me; strong bulls of Bashan
encircle me. Roaring lions tearing their prey open their mouths
wide against me. I am poured out like water, and all my bones are
out of joint. My heart has turned to wax; it has melted away
within me. My strength is dried up like a potsherd, and my tongue
sticks to the roof of my mouth . . . they have pierced my hands and
my feet. I can count all my bones; people stare and gloat over me.
They divide my garments among them and cast lots for my
clothing . . .'[22]

Seeing but not Seeing – Hearing but not Hearing

As Christians of gentile origin we are apt to become over-
familiar with these portions of scripture without recognising
their full and initial significance. Many of us have two blind
spots. Firstly, we see the Old Testament with hindsight and so
we lack understanding of the struggles, the unbelief, the testings
and the victories at each particular stage of revelation and
growth. It is like hearing the life-testimony of a man that God
has used in a remarkable manner. The audience is aware of the
great faith of this man but as he recalls his conversion experience
years ago and recounts the details of stages in his growth – the
early steps of faith, the feeling of uncertainty, the incidents of
doubt and unbelief, the searching for God and crying out to Him
when seemingly He didn't hear, his failures and his sin – somehow the reality of those details do not register because the
audience has only known him as a great man of God.

We have not always read scripture noting to whom it was
addressed and by whom it was written, realising that its content
applied to that particular audience and that promises made

applied only to the party with whom they were made. We are blinded to the full truth of scripture if we fail to recognise these two important points. Failure to do so has resulted in serious error in the Church, as we will demonstrate.

Secondly, we often fail to understand not only that each stage of revelation was given to the Jewish people, but also we fail to grasp what the significance of each stage of the revelation meant to the discerning Jew. As a result we have identified these passages with Jesus our Saviour and Lord but wrested Jesus from His Jewishness and seen Him as a gentile. This in turn has made it easier to reject the Jewish people. This weakness has also rendered ineffective through the centuries much Christian witness to the Jewish people, separating Christians and Jews rather than uniting them. We need to hear and understand Jesus' statement:

'*Salvation is from the Jews.*'[23]

Awaiting the Jewish King

Failing to recognise Jesus' Jewishness also affects our understanding of God's purposes both today and in the future.

We have discovered that Jesus was born to be King, and to rule from the throne of David. Both Isaiah and Jeremiah[24] describe the age in which Jesus will reign, when there is both peace and justice of an order that neither we nor the world have ever experienced. In the book of Revelation, He is described as 'the ruler of the kings of the earth', 'Lord of lords and King of kings'. He is also named 'the Lamb'[25], identifying Him as the One who atoned for sin. In other words, this King is Jewish.

It is important for us to notice that on the occasion when the apostles questioned the risen Jesus about when He was going to restore the kingdom to Israel,[26] Jesus did not correct their thinking about such a restored Jewish kingdom but rather explained that this was **not the time**. He then instructed them as to what they should be doing in the meantime.

Those Jews recognised Jesus as their King. On the occasion of Jesus' circumcision in the Temple, the elderly Simeon recognised Him as destined to be Israel's ruler[27]. At the same time, the prophetess, Anna, recognised Jesus to be Israel's Redeemer. Philip knew Jesus to be the one 'Moses wrote about in the Law'. Nathanael confessed to Jesus, 'You are the King of Israel'[28].

29

The large Jewish crowd that gathered in Jerusalem for Passover shouted to Jesus, 'Blessed is the King of Israel!'[29]. Paul, in writing to Timothy, referred to Jesus as 'the only Ruler, the King of kings and the Lord of lords.'[30]

Not only Jews but also gentiles recognised Jesus to be Israel's King. Wise men travelled a considerable distance from the east to worship the Jewish King[31]. Pilate was so convinced of Jesus' kingship that he ordered it to be written over His head upon the Cross – 'Jesus of Nazareth, the King of the Jews'[32] and to be sure all could read it he had it written in Aramaic, Latin and Greek!

Jesus' response to Pilate's questioning seals the truth.

'My kingdom is not of this world . . . But now my kingdom is from another place.' 'You are a king, then?' said Pilate. Jesus answered, 'You are right in saying I am a king. In fact, for this reason I was born, and for this I came into the world, to testify to the truth. Everyone on the side of truth listens to me.'[33]

Zechariah tells us that King Jesus will return to the Mount of Olives,

'Then the Lord will go out and fight against those nations, as he fights in the day of battle. On that day his feet will stand on the Mount of Olives, east of Jerusalem, and the Mount of Olives will be split in two from east to west, forming a great valley, with half of the mountain moving north and half moving south.'[34]

Zechariah also tells us how the gentile nations will acknowledge the King of the Jews,

'Then the survivors from all the nations that have attacked Jerusalem will go up year after year to worship the King, the Lord Almighty, and to celebrate the Feast of Tabernacles. If any of the peoples of the earth do not go up to Jerusalem to worship the King, the Lord Almighty, they will have no rain . . .'[35]

Jesus even tells us that the Jewish people will be ready to greet their King with the Jewish greeting,

'Blessed is he who comes in the name of the Lord.'[36]

Rich Roots

Many Christians are not aware that the roots of their faith are Jewish. An understanding of the gospel is shallow if it dis-

regards this fact with all that God had prepared for the coming of the Redeemer – Jesus.

When a seed begins to grow it first puts down its unseen root. The root grows down into the soil unnoticed. Then the stem develops upward where we can see growth. But the health of that stem depends totally upon the sound, well established root system. Only this principle can produce a sturdy tree.

Jesus appeared on earth as a tree of sound root structure,

> 'As the terebinth and oak leave stumps when they are cut down, so the holy seed will be the stump in the land . . . A shoot will come up from the stump of Jesse; from his roots a Branch will bear fruit. The Spirit of the Lord will rest on him . . .'[37]

We must be very careful not to see Jesus as **separate** from the 'tree' of which He is, humanly speaking, a part. Paul's statements concerning the root further stress its importance. 'If the root is holy, so are the branches'; conversely the branches can only be holy if the root is holy. 'The nourishing sap comes from the olive root', which means that the entire tree is dependent upon the quality of food which the root provides[38]

To an observant Jew, Paul's statement is clear. God had commanded the Jewish people,

> 'When you come into the land into which I bring you, then it shall be, that, when you eat of the bread of the land, you shall offer up a gift to the Lord. You shall offer up a cake of the first of your dough for a gift: as you do the gift of the threshing floor, so shall you set it apart.'[39]

Even today an orthodox Jewish woman takes a portion of the bread she has prepared and puts it in her oven where she burns it to a cinder. That is God's portion and represents the portion that the ancient Jewish woman took to the Temple priest. The whole loaf is made holy as a result of giving to God His portion.

In addressing the gentiles Paul uses this practice to illustrate their dependence upon their Jewish roots, especially pointing out that their holiness is totally dependent upon their relationship with Jesus,

> 'If the part of the dough offered as firstfruits is holy, then the whole batch is holy; if the root is holy, so are the branches.'[40]

31

Notes

1. *Luke 2:4.*
2. *Matthew 2:2.*
3. *Luke 2:21.*
4. *Exodus 13:2.*
5. *Luke 2:27.*
6. *Luke 2:39.*
7. *Luke 2:41.*
8. Lapide, P.E., *The Last Three Popes and the Jews*, p.17, 18.
9. *Luke 4:16.*
10. *John 7:37–38.*
11. *Luke 8:44* Amplified Bible.
12. *Numbers 15:38–39.*
13. *Genesis 3:15* RSV.
14. *Genesis 49:9–10.*
15. *Leviticus 17:11.*
16. *Deuteronomy 18:15.*
17. *Isaiah 7:14.*
18. *Isaiah 9:6–7.*
19. *Micah 5:2.*
20. *Isaiah 11:1.*
21. *Isaiah 53:2–12.*
22. *Psalm 22.*
23. *John 4:22.*
24. *Isaiah 11:2–10, Jeremiah 23:5–6.*
25. *Revelation 1:5, 17:14, 19:16, 17:14.*
26. *Acts 1:6.*
27. *Luke 2:29–32, 34–35.*
28. *John 1:45, 49.*
29. *John 12:14.*
30. *1 Timothy 6:15.*
31. *Matthew 2:2.*
32. *John 19:19.*
33. *John 18:36–37.*
34. *Zechariah 14:3–4.*
35. *Zechariah 14:16–17.*
36. *Matthew 23:39, Psalm 118:26.*
37. *Isaiah 6:13, 11:1.*
38. *Romans 11:16, 17.*
39. *Numbers 15:19–20* (The Jerusalem Bible).
40. *Romans 11:16.*

Recommended reading

1. *Jesus was a Jew* Arnold Fruchtenbaum.
2. *The Life and Times of Jesus the Messiah* Alfred Edersheim.
3. *The Last Three Popes and the Jews* Pinchas E. Lapide.

3

Members of the Commonwealth of Israel

(*Ephesians* 2:12)

'Christ is the head of the church, his body, of which he is the Saviour,' wrote Paul.[1]

Can we claim to belong to the Head without identifying with the Jewish nature of the Head? Today that is essentially what the Church has done. We have reached a point where we claim a rich inheritance through our privileged relationship with the Head, but usurp the rights of those who are Jewish.

It is true most will say, 'The Jews may accept salvation just as we do.' The history of the Church has shown this to mean that the Jew is required to renounce his Jewishness in order to become a Christian. In other words, the Jew becomes a Gentile Christian. Is that in line with the teaching of Scripture?

Paul writes about this very problem to the young church in Ephesus reminding them of their past,

> '*Remember that you were at that time separated from Christ, alienated from the commonwealth of Israel, and strangers to the convenants of promise, having no hope and without God in the world. But now in Christ Jesus you who once were far off have been brought near in the blood of Christ.*'[2]

Paul is clearly stating that the gentiles, before they knew Christ, were 'alienated from the commonwealth of Israel'. In New Zealand we know what it is to be a member of a 'commonwealth'. We are members of the British Commonwealth. The word can be broken up – 'common': shared ownership; 'wealth': that which is owned, – possessions commonly owned. We have enjoyed trade privileges with Britain, freedom of movement and the opportunity to work in Britain, while still retaining our New Zealand independence.

Before going further we have to identify the 'Israel' of the commonwealth of which we have become members. Paul makes the statement,

'Not all who are descended from Israel are Israel. Nor because they are his descendants are they all Abraham's children.'[3]

Being able to trace back natural lineage to Abraham does not, in itself, qualify a person to be regarded as of 'Israel'. The qualification is restricted to those 'who are the children of promise who are regarded as Abraham's offspring'[4]. Those qualifying for this group are obviously fewer in number than the group who simply are natural descendants of Abraham.

Later, Paul refers to Elijah's experience when he thought he was the only faithful Israelite remaining. Although God had reserved for Himself 7,000 faithful Israelites, it is apparent that this was only a small group compared to the total population of Israel.[5]

These smaller groups of Jewish people are described in scripture as 'the remnant'. In Elijah's day the remnant must have been inconspicuous, judging from his ignorance of their existence. This quietness, which is characteristic of the remnant, is not indicative of a poor quality – reflecting indifference, but rather a quiet, steady confidence in their God: it is a sign of their strength.

Peter, whose ministry was as an apostle to the Jews[6] wrote to the Jews, 'the elect exiles of the dispersion'[7], that the nation as a whole failed but the elect within the nation did not fail – these are the remnant.[8]

Paul is in agreement, 'So too, at the present time there is a remnant chosen by grace'[9] – the true Israel.

Gentiles: Foreigners and Aliens

It is very important for us to understand the extent of the gentiles', separation. 'Gentile' is the Greek word of the Hebrew equivalent 'goyim', meaning the people of the nations, or **anybody** who is **not** Jewish. We will study scripture and then Jewish writing to grasp the totality of this separation.

Jeremiah, in declaring the word of the Lord, rebukes Israel for changing their God,

'Has a nation ever changed its gods? (Yet they are not gods at all.) But my people have exchanged their Glory for worthless idols. Be appalled at this, O heavens, and shudder with great horror,' declares the Lord.'[10]

The point is absolutely clear – **only those belonging to Israel**

knew God while everybody else, that is the gentiles, were
idol-worshipping pagans. 'The nations' and 'the heathen'
were interchangeable terms.

Nehemiah reflects the Jewish attitude towards the gentiles,

> 'Should you not walk in the fear of our God because of the
> reproach of the nations, our enemies?'[11]

The Psalmist presents to us the confusion and helplessness of
the gentile nations in their opposition to God,

> 'Why are the nations in an uproar, and the peoples devising a vain
> thing? The kings of the earth take their stand, and the rulers take
> counsel together against the Lord and against His Anointed: "Let
> us tear their fetters apart, and cast away their cords from us!"'[12]
> 'The nations have sunk down in the pit which they have made; in
> the net which they hid, their own foot has been caught . . . the
> wicked will return to Sheol, even the nations who forget God.'[13]

Ezra described 'the impurity of the nations of the land'.[14]
Joshua reports God's command to kill all the heathen in Canaan
rather than to allow their survival in Israel's Promised Land –
only then was peace and prosperity promised Israel. Moses
forbade inter-marriage with the heathen peoples[15]

**Constantly throughout the Old Testament the nation of
Israel is contrasted with the gentile nations to emphasise
God's unique purpose for Israel, and to offer hope to the
gentile nations through Israel.** God's initial call to Abraham
promised,

> 'In you all the families of the earth shall be blessed.'[16]

Human Prejudice

Dr Alfred Edersheim, the Jewish author, in his monumental
study, 'The Life and Times of Jesus the Messiah' summarises
ancient Jewish writings concerning Jewish attitudes towards
gentiles during the New Testament period,

> 'In truth the bitter hatred which the Jew bore to the Gentile
> can only be explained from the estimate entertained of his
> character. The most vile, and even unnatural crimes were
> imputed to them. It was not safe to leave cattle in their
> charge, to allow their women to nurse infants, or their physi-
> cians to attend the sick, nor to walk in their company,

35

without taking precautions against sudden and unprovoked attacks. They should, as far as possible, be altogether avoided, except in cases of necessity or for the sake of business. They and theirs were defiled; their houses unclean, as containing idols or things dedicated to them; their feasts, their joyous occasions, their very contact, was polluted by idolatry. And there was no security: if a heathen were left alone in a room, that he might not, in wantonness or by carelessness, defile the wine or meat on the table, or the oil and wheat in the store. Under such circumstances, therefore, everything must be regarded as having been rendered unclean. Three days before a heathen festival (according to some, also three days after) every business transaction with them was prohibited, for fear of giving either help or pleasure. Jews were to avoid passing through a city where there was an idolatrous feast – nay, they were not even to sit down within the shadow of a tree dedicated to idol-worship. Its wood was polluted; if used in baking, the bread was unclean; if a shuttle had been made of it, not only was all cloth woven on it forbidden, but if such had been inadvertently mixed with other pieces of cloth, or a garment made from it placed with other garments, the whole became unclean. Jewish workmen were not to assist in building basilicas, nor stadia, nor places where judicial sentences were pronounced by the heathen. Of course, it was not lawful to let houses or fields, nor to sell cattle to them. Milk drawn by a heathen, if a Jew had not been present to watch it, together with bread and oil prepared by them, were unlawful. Their wine was wholly interdicted – the mere touch of a heathen polluted a whole cask; nay, even to put one's nose to heathen wine was strictly prohibited!'[17]

We find in the New Testament examples of gentile awareness of these Jewish attitudes towards them.

In the case of the centurion who desired Jesus to heal his servant, he sent Jewish elders not gentile messengers to Jesus. Secondly, when Jesus came to his house the centurion did not expect Jesus to enter his gentile home.[18]

A Canaanite woman approached Jesus on her daughter's behalf, seeking deliverance. Her persistence attracted Jesus' attention. Jesus' reply,

'It is not right to take the children's bread and toss it to their dogs' is a recognition that she, a gentile woman is seeking something that belongs to the Jewish people.[19]

Peter is shown all the unclean animals which are used to symbolise the gentiles. Peter's reluctance to obey the Lord's command to eat of them shows us his desire to be obedient to the Law of Moses. He had yet to understand how the promise to Abraham was to be fulfilled.

Paul's description of a gentile as a 'foreigner' and an 'alien' before becoming a member of the commonwealth of Israel is therefore not surprising. A 'foreigner' belongs to another people of different thinking and culture. Today 'alien' often refers to one from a different world or planet, stressing his difference from us as absolutely different in every conceivable way to the point of unfriendliness.

This is how the Jewish people looked upon gentiles, as totally different and inferior in their manner of life, morals, gods, language and attitudes.

No Partiality with God

God's purpose with Israel had always been that they who were called out of the world, would reflect God's glory and so influence the nations for God. Significant examples of gentiles who have been drawn to the God of Israel are: Rahab of Jericho, who protected the Jewish spies in the land and so was blessed by becoming a member of the commonwealth of Israel: and Ruth, the Moabitess, who accepted as her own Naomi's people and Naomi's God and later married Boaz the Jew. Both Rahab and Ruth are included in the royal line of David.[20] There is ample evidence of widespread conversion of gentiles to Judaism during the Old Testament period, including members of the royal families of Greece and Rome. Isaiah bears witness to the fact that not only are these gentiles 'joined to the Lord' but that God guarantees them their security,

> *'Let not the foreigner who has joined himself to the Lord say, "The Lord will surely exclude me from this people." And let not any eunuch complain, "I am only a dry tree." For this is what the Lord says: "To the eunuchs who keep my Sabbaths, who choose what pleases me and hold fast to my covenant – to them I will give within my temple and its walls a memorial and a name better than*

sons and daughters; I will give them an everlasting name that will not be cut off. And foreigners who bind themselves to the Lord to serve him, to love the name of the Lord, and to worship him, all who keep the Sabbath without desecrating it and who hold fast to my covenant – these I will bring to my holy mountain and give them joy in my house of prayer. Their burnt offerings and sacrifices will be accepted on my altar; for my house will be called a house of prayer for all nations." '[21]

Change of Status

A glorious change takes place in our lives when we accept the redeeming work of Jesus at Calvary, when we are united with Christ – we have changed our status in God's eyes. Our status changes from being an 'alien from the commonwealth of Israel' to being included in that commonwealth! When we were aliens we were 'foreigners to the covenants of the promise, without hope.' But through our acceptance of Christ we share in the inheritance of the covenants of promise which were given to Israel!

The Covenants of Promise

Having established that our gentile inheritance lies in our relationship with Israel's remnant and that there is a distinction between Jews and non-Jews within God's purposes, Paul presents the inheritance of the Jewish people,

> 'Theirs is the adoption as sons; theirs the divine glory, the covenants, the receiving of the law, the temple worship and the promises. Theirs are the patriarchs, and from them is traced the human ancestry of Christ, who is God over all, forever praised!'[22]

It is essential that we now understand the content of the covenants to know what is promised the Jewish people, and what is promised to gentiles who are members of the commonwealth of Israel.

(1) In order to do this we need to go back to **God's covenant with Abraham:**

> 'The Lord had said to Abram, "Leave your country, your people and your father's household and go to the land I will show you. I will make you into a great nation and I will bless

38

*you; I will make your name great, and you will be a blessing.
I will bless those who bless you, and whoever curses you I
will curse; and all peoples on earth will be blessed through
you." . . . the Lord appeared to Abram and said, "To your
offspring I will give this land." . . . The Lord said to Abram
after Lot had parted from him, "Lift up your eyes from where
you are and look north and south, east and west. All the land
that you see I will give to you and your offspring forever. I
will make your offspring like the dust of the earth, so that if
anyone could count the dust, then your offspring could be
counted. Go, walk through the length and breadth of the
land, for I am giving it to you." [23]*

God promised blessings to Abraham, to his offspring and
to the gentiles.

Abraham would be the father of a great nation who would
possess the land God allocated them. This land allocation is
obviously very important for God repeats 'to you and your
offspring I will give this land'. Abraham's offspring is the
nation of Israel who are promised an enormous population
that will fill the full extent of the territory Abraham looked
upon but which Israel has never yet totally possessed – even
under Solomon's reign. To the gentiles, spiritual blessing is
promised.

So important is this covenant that God ensures that we have
a complete description of His signing the covenant and
sealing the covenant with Abraham. The report of the signing of the covenant, recorded in Genesis chapter 15, follows
Abraham's request for a sign to confirm that God meant
business in His real estate promise.

Acting upon God's command Abraham prepared the covenant sacrifice. Then God did an extraordinary thing. After
putting Abraham to sleep, He revealed the future of Abraham's descendants and appeared in Shekinah glory to sign
the covenant. This is an unconditional covenant, where God
was the sole signatory. Its fulfilment rests on God's faithfulness alone.

God's signed covenant now has to be sealed. Recorded in
Genesis chapter 17, Abraham is renamed 'exalted father'
and God confirmed the promise of a populous, fruitful
nation which would live in the land formerly promised. An
everlasting covenant between God, Abraham and his

descendants and sealed by circumcision, the God-given sign of the covenant people.

The importance of the covenant is further emphasised when later, God confirms these promises to Isaac, Abraham's promised son[24] and years later to Jacob, Isaac's son.[25]

Returning to Paul's writing,

'*Theirs are the* **patriarchs**, *and from them is traced the human ancestry of Christ, who is God over all*'[26]

And writing of God's election of the Jewish people:

'*As far as election is concerned, they are loved on account of the* **patriarchs**'[27]

The apostle is referring to the promises contained in the covenants God made with Abraham, Isaac and Jacob – the patriarchs.

During the centuries that followed God built on the Abrahamic covenant with four other covenants.

(2) The **Mosaic covenant** or the Law of Moses, recorded in *Exodus 20*:1 through *Deuteronomy 28*:68, is the only conditional covenant. Blessings follow obedience to the Law and cursings follow disobedience. Unlike the other covenants this is not an eternal covenant. They key element of this covenant is the blood sacrifice (*Leviticus 17*:11) preparing the way for an eternal covenant. Its purpose was to make sin obvious.

(3) God reaffirmed the territorial promise of His Abrahamic covenant in the **Palestinian covenant** in *Deuteronomy* chapters *29* and *30*. Attention was focussed upon the consequences of disobedience – calamities and dispersion from the land. Repentance would result in restoration to the land.

(4) The seed aspect of the Abrahamic covenant is developed in the **Davidic covenant** which God made with David, who represents the House of David. This covenant singled out one family from whose seed Messiah would come. In *2 Samuel 7*:11–17 God promised David that his son would establish David's kingdom, build a house for God's Name, and that the throne of this son's kingdom would be established forever. God also promised to be a father to David's son whom God will discipline when he strays. At first

reading it appears that *1 Chronicles 17*:10–15 is repetition of this passage.

But, while God makes the same promises of an eternal kingdom, house and throne there is a sharp contrast on two points:

(a) The son spoken of by Samuel will have to be disciplined while there is no mention of disciplining the son referred to by the Chronicler.

(b) Of this son God promises, 'I will set him over *my* house and *my* kingdom forever; his throne will be established forever.'

The promises recorded by Samuel refer to a descendant of David establishing an earthly kingdom, throne and house which will be established forever. However, the Chronicler records **God's promise of His son who will rule from the throne over God's house and kingdom forever**. There is a clear distinction between two of God's sons who will be involved in establishing a throne, building a house, and ruling over a kingdom. History has shown us that Solomon, who had to be disciplined, fulfilled the first function and the second will be fulfilled by Israel's Messiah.

(5) In the fifth covenant – the **New covenant** – God and Israel are involved (*Jeremiah 31*:31–34). This is amplification of the spiritual blessing of the Abrahamic covenant which is made with the houses of Israel and Judah. It is distinct from the Mosaic covenant in which God demanded righteousness from the Jewish people but never gave them the power to keep it. This unconditional covenant replaces that temporary conditional covenant, promising the nation spiritual regeneration, the forgiveness of sin, and a relationship where all in Israel will know God.

Through this covenant the gentiles receive the spiritual blessings promised in the Abrahamic covenant and it is to this covenant that Jesus refers:

'This is my blood of the new covenant, which is poured out for many for the forgiveness of sins.'[28]

While the Mosaic covenant served to keep the Jewish people distinct by controlling their food, clothing and working habits,

41

it also functioned as a 'barrier' or 'dividing wall of hostility' separating the gentiles from the privileges of the Jewish spiritual blessings. As we have seen, throughout the Old Testament period the only way a gentile could receive the spiritual blessings provided by the Jewish covenants was to become a proselyte to Judaism by submission to the Law, by circumcision and living as a Jew was required to live. Paul is now saying that with this 'dividing wall of hostility'[29] destroyed, gentiles can now enjoy the spiritual blessings on the basis of faith.

We dare not underestimate the importance God places on these covenants and must heed His faithfulness to them:

> *'He remembers his covenant forever, the word he commanded, for a thousand generations, the covenant he made with Abraham, the oath he swore to Isaac. He confirmed it to Jacob as a decree, to Israel as an everlasting covenant: 'To you I will give the land of Canaan as the portion you will inherit'* . . . *He allowed no-one to oppress them; for their sake he rebuked kings: "Do not touch my anointed ones; do my prophets no harm."'*[30]

A New Creation

When the gentile, or the non-Jew, finds peace in Jesus, he is made 'one' with Israel's remnant, 'For He Himself is our peace, who made both groups into one, and broke down the barrier of the dividing wall . . .'[31]. What does this oneness mean? Often unity in the church has been interpreted as a bland all-together-ness, all looking the same.

School boards have instituted the system of pupils wearing uniforms to avoid obvious discrimination between the rich and the poor. They try to make all the pupils look the same. The church seems to expect a similar uniformity. Such thinking is taken to the extreme where Jews have been expected to become gentiles – in character and thinking. This is not scriptural unity as with the relationship of Jews and gentiles.

When we return to the Hebrew word for 'one' the difficulty of understanding is immediately overcome. The scripture spoken daily by every orthodox Jew,

> *'Hear, O Israel: The Lord our God, the Lord is one.'*[32]
> 'Shma Israel Adonai Elohenu Adonai Ehad'

The word 'Elohenu' is plural, meaning 'Gods' – as in the royal 'we'. Consequently the word 'one', 'ehad', is also plural. This word 'ehad' is used 90 times in the Old Testament as a composite unity. In *Genesis 2:24* we read of a man and his wife becoming 'one flesh' (bossa ehad). From Canaan they brought 'a single cluster of grapes' (eshcol ehad), *Numbers 13:23*. We read of Israel 'together and united as one man against the city' (ish ehad), *Judges 20:11*.

In *Ephesians 5*, Paul writes about this composite unity regarding the marriage relationship. The husband is given a certain nature and the wife has a complementary nature. Marriage is a close relationship where the two partners are one and the relationship is enriched by what each contributes. Then at the conclusion of the passage Paul states,

> 'This is a profound mystery – but I am talking about Christ and the church.'[33]

The marriage relationship typifies the relationship between Christ and His Church, and similarly applies to the relationships within the Church. So that when Paul speaks of the new relationship between the gentile believer and Israel he says, concerning Jesus:

> 'His purpose was to create in himself one new man out of the two . . .'[34]

Members of the Household

Paul continues His explanation,

> Now therefore ye are no more strangers and foreigners, but fellow citizens with the saints, and of the household of God; and are built upon the foundation of the apostles and prophets; Jesus Christ himself being the chief corner stone; in whom all the building fitly framed together groweth unto an holy temple in the Lord: in whom ye also are builded together for an habitation of God through the Spirit.'[35]

Previously Paul had said that by reconciliation with Christ a gentile becomes a member of the commonwealth of Israel, here he is saying that when we become members of the commonwealth of Israel we become 'members of God's household'. The relationship with Israel is even more intimate.

In a household the members are closely knit together. When one joins a household one is joining a body of people that already exists and is already knit together. Membership in such a body brings privilege with it, and requires adjustment to the life of that established household. **A new member cannot come in and expect to change all that is established according to his whims and fancies. Rather he adapts to fit into the household, and in doing so the newcomer shares in all the advantages and security that have developed before his admission.**

Jewish Foundations

Paul teaches us that the gentiles who are 'fellow citizens' with 'God's people', the Jews, are 'built on the foundation of the apostles and prophets with Christ Jesus himself as the chief cornerstone.' He had said previously that gentile believers are changed in status from 'foreigners and aliens' to members of the commonwealth of Israel. He goes on to describe Israel's solid foundation.

Firstly, the **apostles**, each one a devout Jew, who came under a dynamic power that drew thousands of devout Jews into an understanding of faith in the resurrected Jesus of Nazareth that absolutely transformed their world.

Secondly, the **prophets**, Jewish men of God spanning centuries, fearlessly spoke forth God's will and purpose – calling Jewish people to deepen their relationship with God. They define purity, offer hope, foretell events of the ages to come and make known the Messiah of Israel.

Thirdly, the **Messiah*** is the chief cornerstone through whom all is created, in whom everything is held together, by whom all knowledge is given, and without whom nothing can exist. These three make up the mighty foundation of the commonwealth of Israel of which we gentiles are privileged to become citizens. We are 'raised up with Christ and seated with Him in the heavenly realms in Christ Jesus, in order that in the coming ages He might show the incomparable riches of His grace, expressed in His kindness to us in Christ Jesus.'[36]

---

* Messiah is the Hebrew word for anointed One. Most translations of the Bible use the equivalent Greek word 'Christ'. Jewish people recognise Messiah but 'Christ' is a gentile word.

Notes

1. *Ephesians* 5:23.
2. *Ephesians* 2:12–13. R.S.V.
3. *Romans* 9:6–7.
4. *Romans* 9:8.
5. *Romans* 11:2–5.
6. *Galatians* 2:8.
7. *1 Peter* l:1.
8. *1 Peter* 2:4–8.
9. *Romans* 11:5.
10. *Jeremiah* 2:11–12.
11. *Nehemiah* 5:9 NASB.
12. *Psalm* 2:1–3 NASB.
13. *Psalm* 9:15, 17 NASB.
14. *Ezra* 6:21.
15. *Deuteronomy* 7:1–3.
16. *Genesis* 12:3 NASB.
17. Edersheim A. *The Life and Times of Jesus the Messiah, Book 1*, p.91–92.
18. *Luke* 7:1–8.
19. *Matthew* 15:21–27.
20. *Matthew* 1:5.
21. *Isaiah* 56:3–7.
22. *Romans* 9:4–5.
23. *Genesis* 12:1–3, 7; *13*:14–17.
24. *Genesis* 26:2–5, 24.
25. *Genesis* 28:13–15.
26. *Romans* 9:5.
27. *Romans* 11:28.
28. *Matthew* 26:28.
29. *Ephesians* 2:14.
30. *Psalm* 105:8–11, 15.
31. *Ephesians* 2:14 NASB.
32. *Deuteronomy* 6:4.
33. *Ephesians* 5:32.
34. *Ephesians* 2:15.
35. *Ephesians* 2:19–22 A.V.
36. *Ephesians* 2:6–8.

Recommended reading

1. *The Covenants and the Promises*, K.A. McNaughtan.

4

Mysteries Revealed

(Ephesians 3:3)

'This mystery is that, through the gospel, the Gentiles are heirs together with Israel.'

Although God had said many times to the Jewish people that they would be a light to the gentile nations, He kept secret from His people details of His provision for the gentiles, and the future relationship of His chosen people with them. The great challenge Paul faced was that God had selected him to reveal mysteries never before made known to man. When Paul revealed what was shown to him many did not believe or understand him. Today there are many of us who still do not believe or understand some of those same truths which Paul labours to explain,

> *'In reading this, then, you will be able to understand my insight into the mystery of Christ, which was not made known to men in other generations as it has now been revealed by the Spirit to God's holy apostles and prophets. This mystery is that through the gospel the Gentiles are heirs together with Israel, members together of one body, and sharers together in the promise in Christ Jesus . . . to make plain to everyone the administration of this mystery, which for ages past was kept hidden in God, who created all things. His intent was that now, through the church, the manifold wisdom of God should be made known to the rulers and authorities in the heavenly realms, according to his eternal purpose which he accomplished in Christ Jesus our Lord. In him and through faith in him we may approach God with freedom and confidence.'[1]*

As we have discovered, God prepared a way for the coming of Jesus into the world, through Israel, of which He is a part. At the same time, God prepared a way through the work of Jesus for non-Jewish people, gentiles, to become a part of Israel. **This does not make gentiles Jewish any more than it makes Jews** into gentiles. When the two become 'one man' we see an expression of spiritual unity where all that has separated them has been removed. They become members of 'one body', the Church, each making his distinct contribution.

In order to see clearly the purpose of the Church we need to look back to our origin. God reminded Israel of this,

> 'Listen to me, you who pursue righteousness, who seek the Lord: Look to the rock from which you were hewn, and to the quarry from which you were dug.'[2]

Israel needed to be reminded then, and the Church needs to be reminded now, that Abraham, the man separated unto God, foreshadows a people separated unto God. Both the man and the people by faith and obedience will inherit the promise. **The covenant with Abraham is not yet fulfilled but it will reach total fulfillment when that new man inherits the Kingdom of God.**

Paul's Intense Anguish for his Brothers

Paul, who described himself as 'advancing in Judaism beyond many Jews of my own age'[3], writes out of great anguish for his Jewish brethren,

> 'I have great sorrow and unceasing anguish in my heart. For I could wish that I myself were cursed and cut off from Christ for the sake of my brothers, those of my own race, the people of Israel.'[4]

Paul's anguish comes from the state of his brothers,

> 'It is not as though God's word had failed. For not all who are descended from Israel are Israel. Nor because they are his descendants are they all Abraham's children . . . Israel who pursued a law of righteousness, has not attained it . . . because they pursued it not by faith but as if it were by works.'[5]

The Apostle is writing to a confused church composed of Christian Jews and Christian Gentiles, each group claiming advantages over the other. Throughout this letter Paul is travailing to explain that all men are sinful and in need of redemption. While the Jewish people cannot simply claim superiority because God has favoured them by giving them the covenants of promise, the Gentiles need to recognise their own indebtedness to Israel and also that God has not yet fulfilled His purpose in the Jewish people,

> *'I ask then, did God reject his people? By no means! . . . Again I ask, did they stumble so as to fall beyond recovery? Not at all!'*[6]

Paul directs the attention of both Israel and the Church to the great hope revealed by God that lies ahead in the one man in the one body. That hope will be fully realised when both Israel and the Church have appropriated the fullness of the covenants of promise. Meantime a season of 'hardening in part' is upon Israel.

Israel Hardened in Part

Paul reveals the reason for Israel's partial response to Jesus as Messiah,

> *'That which Israel is seeking for, it has not obtained, but those who were chosen obtained it, and the rest were hardened . . . I do not want you, brethren, to be uninformed of this mystery, lest you be wise in your own estimation, that a partial hardening has happened to Israel until the fullness of the Gentiles has come in; and thus all Israel will be saved.'*[7]

We learn from this that there is to be a period in history when God is going to provide opportunities for the gentiles to come into fullness of faith. But in revealing this truth **Paul cautions the gentiles about becoming conceited now that they are receiving God's rich blessings**. Paul, deeply aware of human nature and the proud arrogance that gentiles are already displaying in their attitude towards Israel, goes out of his way to emphasise that this opportunity for the gentiles is only for a restricted period of time, and even gives the reason why God has permitted the gentiles this privilege of salvation,

> *'Because of their transgression, **salvation has come to the Gentiles to make Israel envious**. But if their transgression means riches for the world, and their loss means riches for the Gentiles, how much greater riches will their fullness bring!'*[8]

Not only has God graciously offered this special opportunity to the gentiles but He declares His purpose is that gentiles are to make Israel **envious** of their redemption privilege. We gentiles should be so blessed by our acceptance into the commonwealth of Israel, being made heirs of the covenants of promise given to Israel, that we not only recognise God's special place for Israel, but we also want to embrace Israel, and to encourage her into her God ordained inheritance.

God also tells us that there will be a time when Israel will come into the fullness of her inheritance and bring rich blessing to the world and final fulfilment of God's promise to Abraham.

Paul goes even further in making his point, addressed to gentiles, concerning the inheritance of Israel and the gentiles,

> *'As far as the gospel is concerned, they are enemies on your account; but as far as election is concerned, they are loved on account of the patriarchs, for God's gifts and his call are irrevocable.'*[9]

God's covenant with the patriarchs still stands no matter what man does – God is always faithful! God will bring Israel into the inheritance He has purposed for them and no man or circumstance will thwart God's purpose.

We are soberly reminded of God's graciousness towards us without which we would be nothing,

> *'Just as you who were at one time disobedient to God have now received mercy as a result of their disobedience, so they too have now become disobedient in order that they too may now receive mercy as a result of God's mercy to you. For God has bound all men over to disobedience so that he may have mercy on them all.'*[10]

God's Sovereignty

Before revealing the truth of these mysteries Paul carefully prefaces the section with the fact of God's sovereignty which he illustrates with God's choice of Jacob in preference to Esau,

> *'Rebecca's children had one and the same father, our father Isaac. Yet, before the twins were born or had done anything good or bad – in order that God's purpose in election might stand: not by works but by him who calls – she was told, "The older will serve the younger." Just as it is written: Jacob I loved, but Esau I hated.'*[11]

Anyone who knows Middle Eastern culture realises that a younger son never takes precedence over an older son – it just

50

does not happen! But God has done just that and His decision was made before the boys' birth. Paul concludes,

> 'It does not, therefore, depend on man's desire or effort, but on God's mercy . . . Therefore God has mercy on whom he wants to have mercy, and he hardens whom he wants to harden.'[12]

Prior to entering the Promised Land Moses strengthens Israel's faith by reminding them of God's sovereignty in their lives and His faithfulness to His covenants,

> 'The Lord did not set His love on you nor choose you because you were more in number than any of the peoples, for you were the fewest of all peoples, but because the Lord loved you and kept the oath which He swore to your forefathers, the Lord brought you out by a mighty hand, and redeemed you from the house of slavery, from the hand of Pharoah the king of Egypt. Know therefore that the Lord your God, He is God, **the faithful God who keeps His covenant** and His lovingkindness to a thousandth generation with those who love Him and keep His commandments; but repays those who hate Him to their faces, to destroy them . . .'[13]

Paul, like Moses before him, is striving to bring understanding of God's purpose for His people.

The Rich Root of the Olive Tree

At the climax of his teaching Paul uses the Olive tree as a symbol. A tree common to all Middle East countries and significant for its persistent life – it does not die! This stresses the certainty of God's purposes with His people.

Some of the olive branches have been broken off, these represent Israelites who have not received the promise. Wild olive shoots have been grafted in among natural olive branches. These grafted in wild olive shoots represent gentiles who have accepted the promises of God, and they are receiving their nourishment from the root of the olive tree.

Gentiles are warned against boasting over being grafted in because nourishment comes from the roots, not the branches. It is important that the gentiles recognise that the broken-off branches are broken off so that gentiles could be grafted in, and that the breaking off was caused by unbelief. Gentiles are again warned that they are grafted in by faith, and they do well to learn the lesson from the removal of the natural branches in case their arrogance in turn results in their own removal.

51

'I am talking to you gentiles . . . If the root is holy, so are the branches. If some of the branches have been broken off, and you, though a wild olive shoot, have been grafted in among the others and now share in the nourishing sap from the olive root, do not boast over those branches. If you do, consider this: You do not support the root, but the root supports you. You will say then, "Branches were broken off so that I could be grafted in. Granted. **But they were broken off because of unbelief, and you stand by faith. Do not be arrogant, but be afraid. For if God did not spare the natural branches, he will not spare you either.** *Consider therefore the kindness and sternness of God: sternness to those who fell, but kindness to you, provided that you continue in his kindness. Otherwise, you also will be cut off."'[14]*

Grafting is an excitingly creative activity. Successful grafting is carried out when the sap is flowing in the tree. A small, tender shoot is taken, its stem sharpened until the growth cells under the bark are exposed and the microscopic cells that convey the food to the plant are clean and exposed. This shoot is then gently fitted into a cut-away branch on the tree, where the natural branch has been removed, so that the layer of growing cells are matched and the food-conveying cells are matched. This join is bound up so that air and water cannot reach it. The grafted in shoot is fragile, needing protection against knocks, and is totally dependent upon the natural tree for its sustenance.

When I was a child my father grafted into a sturmer apple tree shoots from a granny-smith and a golden delicious apple tree. In time, these grew – producing three varieties of apple, each in its own season, on the one tree. We were picking sturmers, granny-smiths and golden delicious off the same tree! The granny-smiths and the golden delicious were only branches and they were totally dependent upon a sturmer trunk and roots which in turn provided the nourishment they depended upon.

This is exactly what Paul is saying. The shoot and its subsequent fruit, which appears in its own season, is dependent upon the trunk and roots for nourishment. **The gentiles, grafted in, are totally dependent upon the Israel of promise**,

'Theirs is the adoption as sons; theirs the divine glory, the covenants, the receiving of the law, the temple worship and the promises. Theirs are the patriarchs, and from them is traced the human ancestry of Christ, who is God over all, forever praised!'[15]

In the gospels we read of a Roman centurion who came to Jesus for healing on behalf of his servant. Jewish elders approached Jesus giving the centurion a reference: 'This man deserves to have you do this, because he loves our nation and has built our synagogue.'[16] Commentators believe this is the same centurion recorded in *Acts 10* where he is named, Cornelius, who, with his household, were the first gentiles to be grafted in to the Olive tree. An important characteristic of Cornelius' faith was his love for Israel.

An exciting future lies ahead:

> *'And if they do not persist in unbelief, they will be grafted in, for God is able to graft them in again. After all, if you were cut out of an olive tree that is wild by nature, and contrary to nature were grafted into a cultivated olive tree, **how much more readily will these, the natural branches, be grafted into their own olive tree!**'*[17]

As we witness the power of Christ at work among the gentile members of His Church, as thousands are today being grafted into the olive tree, we must remember we are seeing Him graft contrary to nature, wild olive branches into a natural tree that is flourishing. How much easier it will be for God to graft back the natural branches into the natural tree and how much more will that olive tree flourish!

It is not surprising that when I have met Jewish people who have worshipped the God of Israel and later come to receive the promise God offers them in Jesus Christ, I have observed in them a depth of understanding that is not found in gentile believers. Of course, it should be so for they are the natural olive branches.

A future event in scripture shows how gentiles will ultimately recognise and be drawn to Jews who have received the promises of God,

> *'This is what the Lord Almighty says: "In those days ten men from all languages and nations will take firm hold of one Jew by the edge of his robe and say, 'Let us go with you, because we have heard that God is with you.'"'*[18]

Notes

1. *Ephesians 3*:4–6, 9–12.
2. *Isaiah 51*:1 NASB.

3. *Galatians 1*:14.
4. *Romans 9*:2–3.
5. *Romans 9*:6–7, 31–32.
6. *Romans 11*:1, 11.
7. *Romans 11*:7, 25–26 NASB.
8. *Romans 11*:11–12.
9. *Romans 11*:28–29.
10. *Romans 11*:30–32.
11. *Romans 9*:10–13.
12. *Romans 9*:16, 18.
13. *Deuteronomy 7*:7–10 NASB.
14. *Romans 11*:16–22.
15. *Romans 9*:4–5.
16. *Luke 7*:4–5.
17. *Romans 11*:23–24.
18. *Zechariah 8*:23.

Recommended reading

1. *The Everlasting Nation and Their Coming King*, Samuel Schor.

5

The Synagogue and the Church

It is generally believed that the Church was born (or revealed) on the glorious day of Pentecost recorded in *Acts*, chapter 2. God graciously visited the Jewish people as they gathered from the extremities of the Roman Empire, in the Temple in Jerusalem, to offer thanks for His provision of the gathered-in harvest. The dynamic of faith released within these faithful Jews created a growing body of believers who were soon accused of 'turning the world upside down'!

The 120 Jews, whose lives had been transformed by Jesus of Nazareth, were immediately joined by another 3,000, and then by another 5,000 Jewish men. Other records state that within 20 years, by A.D. 50, there were over 50,000 Jewish believers in Jesus in Jerusalem alone! By the end of the first century there were more than 1,000,000 Jewish followers of Jesus the Messiah, according to August Neander the 19th century Jewish historian.[1]

Paul, who 'to the Jews became like a Jew, to win the Jews'[2] states,

> *'I am not ashamed of the gospel, because it is the power of God for the salvation of everyone who believes: first for the Jew, then for the Gentile.'*[3]

We must note two very important facts. **These were Jewish people who had received the fullness of the promises of God with the visitation of the Holy Spirit. They did not separate themselves into a new body leaving the synagogue and Temple, cutting themselves off from other Jews to build a church, but saw the new dimension of their faith as a fulfilment of all they had been promised in the Law, the Prophets and the Psalms.**

From the Synagogue emerges the Church

The origins of the New Testament Church can be understood only in relation to the structure and function of the synagogue. It has been suggested by many New Testament commentators and Church historians that the young church emerged as a totally new organisation. This is not correct as we shall demonstrate.

The total destruction of the Temple, and the Jewish exile in Babylon for 70 years, (commencing in 586 B.C.) caused a dramatic upheaval in Jewish life. The sacrifices and oblations, around which their whole life had centred, ceased. The religious leaders developed a religious institution that remains in Judaism until today.

The synagogue, which is Greek for 'assembly', is known in Hebrew as 'bet knesset', the house of the assembly. While it is organised primarily as an institution for teaching, the synagogue became the centre for all Jewish community life and has been responsible for holding Judaism together through the centuries of dispersion among the many nations. The structure which emerged in Babylon is clearly the synagogue of the New Testament period.

The Synagogue Structure

Overseeing the functioning of the synagogue is the **nasi**, or the president, whose role is primarily administrative. He acts as the administrator of the congregation.

The 'skanaim', derived from the Hebrew word 'zaken', meaning 'old' or 'elder', are a group of men who act as 'elders', a role not dependent upon their age but their spiritual maturity. These men are really the spiritual leaders of the synagogue and congregation.

Another group whose function is to teach, derives its name from the Hebrew word for 'man of leisure' – the **'batlahmim'**. Ideally, each synagogue has ten of these men who usually have independent financial means and can therefore devote themselves to constant study and to teaching the congregation.

There is another group of men known in Hebrew as the **'gabet zdaka'**, which means 'those who undertake acts of righteousness'. Their task is to minister to the everyday needs of the community, especially to the widows, orphans and to other special needs.

The **'schlakim'**, those who were sent forth from the synagogue oversight as public announcers, communicated messages to other synagogues and individuals.

The **'bet din'**, which means 'house of judgment', was the court of law in the synagogue before whom offenders appeared for judgment. The kazan, who today functions as the cantor, was the one who after judgment was passed, dealt the punishment. Each synagogue was an autonomous body with its own government and court. Jesus clearly referred to this,

> *'When you are brought before synagogues, rulers and authorities, do not worry about how you will defend yourselves or what you will say, for the Holy Spirit will teach you at that time what you should say.'*[4]

Jesus was referring to the bet din. We can also see here the background to New Testament teaching regarding disagreements among believers,

> *'If your brother sins against you, go and show him his fault, just between the two of you. If he listens to you, you have won your brother over. But if he will not listen, take one or two others along, so that "every matter may be established by the testimony of two or three witnesses." If he refuses to listen to them, tell it to the church . . .'*[5]

The **'meturganaim'** were the interpreters. When the Jewish people were dispersed to the nations they always worshipped in Hebrew so that when the Bible was read it had to be translated into the local language.

The **'mahgeed'**, men gifted in public speaking, travelled among the synagogues – stimulating congregations with their inspiring messages at the president's request. They were not necessarily associated with one particular synagogue. We find occasions in the gospels when Jesus was invited to speak to the congregation – it was in this capacity.

A **Rabbi** could be shared among several small congregations or in the case of a large synagogue there could be several rabbis. We have seen that there are already several spiritual leaders so the rabbi was not the only one fulfilling that role. His wisdom was sought after in matters of the Law and he was needed to supervise conversions. In the synagogue service all the Jewish members are equal as ministers and all can take part.

New Dimensions

Following the day of Pentecost, Luke describes the activities of these Jewish believers in Jesus,

> 'They devoted themselves to the apostles' teaching and to the fellowship, to the breaking of bread and to prayer. Everyone was filled with awe, and many wonders and miraculous signs were done by the apostles. All the believers were together and had everything in common. Selling their possessions and goods, they gave to anyone as he had need. Every day they continued to meet together in the temple courts. They broke bread in their homes and ate together with glad and sincere hearts, praising God and enjoying the favour of all the people. And the Lord added to their number daily those who were being saved.'[6]

These were Jews who saw in their new dimension of faith the fulfilment of the Messianic covenants God had made with Abraham, Isaac and Jacob and they continued their involvement in the Temple and synagogue.

As their numbers grew rapidly the leadership gifts to which they had been accustomed in the synagogue emerged in the embryonic church. We read of this in Paul's writing,

> 'And in the church God has appointed first of all apostles, second prophets, third teachers, then workers of miracles, also those having gifts of healing, those able to help others, those with gifts of administration, and those speaking in different kinds of tongues.'[7]

An 'apostle' is one who is sent, (from the Greek word 'apostolos'). We see the young church sending out men, schlakim, commissioned by the believers to communicate with other groups of believers. Just as the 'sent out ones' were responsible to the synagogue, the apostles were responsible to Jesus on whose behalf they were commissioned.

'Teachers' are equivalent to 'the men of leisure', batlahmim, who spent their time studying the scriptures in readiness to impart their knowledge.

'Evangelist' corresponds to the mahgeed, an able public speaker who visited the synagogues with an inspiring message.

The role of **'pastor'** is that of an elder, skanim. We use the term pastor in quite a loose sense today where his function is not always clearly defined; often the pastor, as we see him today, fulfils the function of the biblical role of **'deacon'**. Deacon comes from the Greek 'diakonia', first mentioned in *Acts 6* when needs of believers were being overlooked. Those appointed to care for these needs were called deacons, modelled on the office of the gabet zdaka in the synagogue and are a helps ministry.

For centuries there have been rabbis who have visited the sick, laying on hands and anointing with oil.

Justin Martyr, one of the notable leaders of the Church during the late first century and early second century (the period following soon after the New Testament period) described the church worship of his day. In this description we can clearly see the pattern of the synagogue,

> 'On Sunday a meeting is held of all who live in the cities and villages and a section is read from the memoirs of the apostles and the writings of the prophets as long as time permits. When the reading is finished, the president, in a discourse, gives the admonition and the exhortation to imitate these noble things. After this we all arise and offer a common prayer and at the close of the prayer, as we have before described, bread and wine and thanks for them are offered, and the congregation answers 'Amen'.
>
> Then the consecrated elements are distributed to each one and partaken of and are then carried by the deacons to the houses of the absent.
>
> The wealthy and the willing then give contributions according to their free will and this collection is deposited with the president who therewith supplies orphans, widows, prisoners, strangers and all who are in want.'[8]

Born Anew

We have seen in chapter 3 the state of the gentiles, totally separated from God without hope or promise, and the opportunity for them to come close to the God of Israel as proselytes. The process of becoming a proselyte involved 'baptism'. **A close look at the baptism of proselytes again demonstrates to us an activity of the synagogue adopted by the church and given a new dimension of meaning.**

There were four categories of proselytes but 'the proselytes of righteousness' were those who fully embraced the God of Israel – they were also referred to as 'perfect Israelites' which means they were Israelites in every respect both as regards duties and privileges. These proselytes are frequently mentioned in the New Testament – in the Authorised Version they are referred to as those who 'fear God', 'religious', 'devout', 'worship God'.[9] Three things were required for the admission of such proselytes: circumcision (mila), baptism (tebhila), and a sacrifice (corban).

It was considered a great thing when a non-Jew 'sought shelter under the wings of the Shekinah' and his change of condition was complete. When the proselyte stepped out of the waters of baptism he was considered as 'born anew'. The Rabbis described it as if he were ' a little child just born' and in another place as 'a child of one day'. This new birth was not 'a birth from above' in the sense of moral or spiritual change, but only as implying a new relationship to God, to Israel, and to his own past, present and future. He was then instructed in the difficulties of his 'new citizenship', particularly regarding his changed status and his past. As a new man, his country, habits, friends and relations were separated from him; the old – with its defilements – was buried in the waters of baptism.

Clearly Jesus had this in mind when replying to Rabbi Nicodemus,

'Unless a man is born again, he cannot see the kingdom of God.'[10]

Paul also had this in his mind when he spoke on baptism,

'What shall we say, then? Shall we go on sinning, so that grace may increase? By no means! We died to sin; how can we live in it any longer? Or don't you know that all of us who were baptised into Christ Jesus were baptised into his death? We were therefore buried with him through baptism into death in order that, just as Christ was raised from the dead through the glory of the Father, we too may live a new life . . . For we know that our old self was crucified with him so that the body of sin might be rendered powerless, that we should no longer be slaves to sin – because anyone who has died has been freed from sin . . . Therefore do not let sin reign in your mortal body so that you obey its evil desires.'[11]

Passover or Easter?

Today many Christians do not realise that **the death and resurrection of Jesus was a precise and accurate fulfilment of the Jewish Passover, a practice commanded by God through Moses and recorded in Exodus 12 and Numbers 9.** Easter was not instituted until the fourth century, when the anti-Jewish thinking among the leaders of the Church led them to make two detrimental changes. They separated the date for celebrating Jesus' death and resurrection from the time Jewish people observed Passover, which was biblical, to a non-biblical date of a pagan festival. The influence of pagan practices and understanding replaced the Jewish, biblical purpose of the event. This marks an ongoing, determined attempt to remove Jewishness from the Church.

It is very significant that the Jewish believers in Jesus continued to celebrate His death and resurrection at Passover as did many non-Jewish believers in Jesus even after the Church leaders separated the observance from the Jewish date.

The instructions in the Law of Moses and the gospel accounts were written for Jews and must be understood as they would have understood them. This principle is fundamental to a right understanding of scripture and would shed light on many scriptures obscure to the gentile mind but very clear to the Jews.

A Jewish writer, Arnold Fruchtenbaum, highlights a vital truth when he explains that the church lacks depth of understanding because of its disregard of the Jewish perspective:

'If this had been the pattern followed by the church throughout the centuries, it could have saved itself a great amount of doctrinal error. For no Jew would have remained in the local church and allowed anyone to challenge the authority of the Scriptures or to deny the Virgin Birth and the Resurrection. The church has lost much in failing to bring the gospel to the Jew.'[12]

The scholar, James Parkes also recognises the important place Jewish members of the Church played in its stability and the weakness it suffered as a result of their being cut off. But that is not all; he records for us a determined effort by the gentile Christians to continue the Jewish biblical practice after Church leaders had legislated otherwise,

'Though there is no evidence of Christianity adopting any practices of post-Christian Judaism, yet relations with contemporary Jews were continual, and are shown by the number of centuries it took to separate the Jewish Passover from the Christian Easter. It was not until the time of Constantine that a formal decision was taken, and **even in later centuries councils had frequently to prohibit Gentile Christians from celebrating Easter on the same day as the Jews celebrated the Passover. In other matters also it is evident that many, apart from Christians of Jewish birth, were powerfully influenced by the teaching and practice of the Synagogue.** Though this provoked the furious denunciation of such bishops as Chrysostom, it is significant that he has no definite moral charges to bring against the Christians who were involved, and it seems to have been fear of Jewish influence which caused his violence more than anything else.'[13]

Notes

1. Neander, A., *History of the Planting and Training of the Christian Church by the Apostles*, volume 1.
2. *1 Corinthians 9*:20.
3. *Romans 1*:16.
4. *Luke 12*:11–12.
5. *Matthew 18*:15–17.
6. *Acts 2*:42–47.
7. *1 Corinthians 12*:27–28.
8. Justin Martyr, *The First Apology* as quoted in *Ante-Nicene Fathers*, vol. 1, p.185–186.
9. *Acts 13*:16, 26, 43, 50; *17*:4, 17; *16*:14; *18*:7.
10. *John 3*:3.
11. *Romans 6*:1–4, 6–7, 12.
12. Fruchtenbaum A., *Hebrew Christianity*, p.95.
13. Parkes J., *The Conflict of the Church and the Synagogue*, p.119.

Recommended reading

1. *Hebrew Christianity*, Arnold Fruchtenbaum.

6

The Separation of the Synagogue and the Church

'The Jews killed Jesus!'

This has been the accusing cry of many Christians down the ages. Such a course of vengeance and bloodshed followed this accusation that a deep stain has marred church history. Little attention was paid to Paul's warnings against the arrogance and pride of gentiles who despised the Jewish people. Although there is some evidence of Christian concern for the Jewish people, the policy has been generally hostile, bringing persecution and intense suffering.

A theology concerning the Jewish people has been built upon their statement at the time of Jesus' trial,

> 'All the people answered, "Let his blood be on us and on our children!"'[1]

A doctrine has been built upon this one verse which ignores all the teaching of Paul and even the words of Jesus, just hours after this trial scene, when He prayed from the Cross for these very people who were crucifying Him:

> 'Jesus said, "Father, forgive them, for they do not know what they are doing."'[2]

Did the Father hear this prayer?

Whose Responsibility?

The responsibility for Jesus' crucifixion is apportioned very carefully by Peter,

> 'Indeed Herod and Pontius Pilate met together with the Gentiles and the people of Israel in this city to conspire against your holy servant Jesus, whom you anointed. They did what your power and will had decided beforehand should happen.'[3]

The responsibility is clearly apportioned:

(1) Some Jewish people were responsible for Jesus' crucifixion.
(2) Herod, Pontius Pilate, the Gentiles, were responsible for Jesus' crucifixion.
(3) Almighty God who had planned this foreordained one and only means of salvation for mankind. In the book of the Revelation we read,

> *'The Lamb that was slain from the creation of the world.'*[4]

It is obvious for us all to see that the sacrificial death of Jesus was in the mind of God before the world was created.

(4) We must also hear what Jesus says concerning His life,

> *'No-one takes it from me, but I lay it down of my **own** accord. I have authority to lay it down and authority to take it up again. This command I received from my Father.'*[5]

(5) For those of us who are believers we need to consider our own personal involvement insofar as Scripture teaches,

> *'He was pierced for **our** transgressions, he was crushed for our iniquities.'*[6]

Parting of the Ways

Many Christians know the times of the early Church only from the pages of the New Testament. Often it comes as a surprise to know that the secular authorities did not distinguish between the Jews within Judaism and the Jews who believed in Jesus. The main body of the believers were all Jews: 3,000 in *Acts* 2:41, 5,000 men in *Acts* 4:4 while many were being added daily to their number. These were all Jews who were receiving salvation, being baptised, and sharing their faith with fellow Jews. We see further in *Acts* that Gentiles were added and so the Gentile numbers grew.

As time progressed the believers became more dispersed throughout the Roman Empire. It became evident that they were separate from the Jews of Judaism, although they were initially seen as a sect of Judaism. Judaism received better acceptance within the Roman Empire than did early Christianity. While it is true that some emperors were harsh towards Jewish people they intensely persecuted Christians. The religion of the Jews enjoyed a privileged place within the Roman Empire generally. Jewish people were able to worship and live according to their Law, provided they did not conflict with Roman requirements.

You will remember the occasion when the Pharisees tried to trap Jesus by asking about paying tax to Caesar and His famous reply, 'Give to Caesar what is Caesar's, and to God what is God's'[7]. The Jewish leaders had always protected this privilege and they feared Jesus might be responsible for their losing it. This is an important part of the reason why the leaders in Jerusalem wanted Jesus removed.

Church growth was phenomenal. If tradition is correct the apostles had reached as far as India in the east and Britain in the north. It was evident that the Church was separate from Judaism and it was harshly treated by the Roman authorities. We see clear evidence of persecution even in the New Testament. This is the reason for John's exile on Patmos Island. The Church operated underground, and it grew because of persecution.

The growing tensions that we see in the gospels between Jesus and the Jewish religious leaders were inherited by the young church. Christianity had been protected as long as it was seen to be part of Judaism but the Church became more and more Gentile in numbers and in its nature. By the middle of the second century the separation was clear.

A prominent 4th century church historian, Eusebius, shows us that even back **in the 2nd century there were church leaders who emphasised their separation from the Jews by moving the date for remembering Jesus' death and resurrection away from the time of the Jewish observance of Passover.** Bishop Polycrates, writing in the 2nd century, concerning keeping the memorial of Jesus' death and resurrection according to the Jewish calendar, states,

'We for our part keep the day scrupulously, without addition or subtraction. For in Asia great luminaries sleep who shall rise again on the day of the Lord's advent, when He is coming with glory from heaven and shall search out all His saints . . . (he lists seven martyrs) . . . All of these kept the fourteenth day of the month as the beginning of the Paschal festival, in accordance with the Gospel, not deviating in the least but following the rule of the Faith. Last of all I too, Polycrates, the least of you all, act according to the tradition of my family, some members of which I have actually followed; for seven of them were bishops and I am the eighth, and my family have always kept the day when the people put away the leaven. So I, my friends, after spending sixty-five years in the Lord's service and conversing with Christians from all parts of the world, and going carefully through all Holy Scripture, am not scared of threats. Better people than I have said: "We must obey God rather than men."'[8]

Polycrates was the leader of a group known as the Quartodecimans, in Asia, who persisted in observing Jesus' death and resurrection at Passover. For many years the popes accepted this stand in Asia until Pope Victor excommunicated the group who then organised themselves into a separate church.[9]

The Jewish Church

This means that the first Christians were Jewish Christians and gentiles that had become 'proselytes', that is, they had converted to Judaism by circumcision and submitting to the Law of Moses. These Jewish Christians had no plan for sharing their new dimension of faith with gentiles, the thought had never crossed their minds. Evidence of this is seen in the manner God spoke to Peter preparing him for the call to Cornelius' house [10]. Peter's absolute amazement that these gentiles should experience the same manifestation of the Spirit of the God of Israel is further evidence that the gentiles had not been considered by the Jewish Christians. The apprehension and concern of the church leaders in Jerusalem regarding Peter's action yet again demonstrates that, until this time, the Church was totally Jewish, with no expectation that it should embrace gentiles other than those who had converted to Judaism.

We need to remember that God was leading His people into a new dimension of faith, revealing new truth, and that the revelation of this new truth was to devout Jews. **After the blessing of Pentecost came the utter surprise that the blessing was to be shared with gentiles who had not previously submitted themselves to circumcision and the Law of Moses.** Now we must remember that Cornelius was not the first gentile to put his faith in the God of Israel – there had been Rahab, Ruth and thousands of others who had all become proselytes. However, Cornelius is described as 'a righteous and God-fearing man who is respected by all the Jewish people' but he was not a proselyte.

That is why this divine revelation was so startling to the church leaders.

As the church expanded during a period of phenomenal growth among the gentiles, we come to the first major problem in the Jewish Church where some taught 'unless you are circumcised, according to the custom taught by Moses, you cannot be saved.'[11] A Council in Jerusalem under the presidency of James, decided against enforcing these requirements, demanding only that they refrain from eating food used in idol worship, and from sexual immorality. They circularised a letter to all the gentile churches informing them of the decision.

While this was satisfactory for the churches in Asia where the congregations were a mixture of Jewish and gentile believers, the churches in Judea consisting of conservative Jewish Christians preferred to observe the Law of Moses,

> *'When they heard this, they praised God. Then they said to Paul:* **"You see, brother, how many thousands of Jews have believed, and all of them are zealous for the law.** *They have been informed that you teach all the Jews who live among the Gentiles to turn away from Moses, telling them not to circumcise their children or live according to our customs.*
>
> *What shall we do? They will certainly hear that you have come, so do what we tell you. There are four men with us who have made a vow. Take these men, join in their purification rites and pay their expenses, so that they can have their heads shaved. Then everybody will know there is no truth in these reports about you, but that you yourself are living in obedience to the law.* **As for the Gentile believers, we have written to them our decision that they should abstain from food sacrificed to idols, from blood, from the meat of strangled animals and from sexual immorality.'**[12]

A Greek text which is translated in verse 20 'many thousands of Jews have believed' reads 'myriads of Jews have believed'. The fact is clear that many more than thousands of Jews came to believe – we quoted above there were over 50,000 Jewish Christians in Jerusalem at the time of the Council.

There was no difference of opinion so far as personal salvation was concerned between those of Jewish and those of gentile background although their expressions of faith and life were very different. We note that they were known by different names. In Antioch the gentile believers came to be known as 'Christians'[13] while the Jewish believers in Jesus were called 'Nazarenes' and described as a sect within Judaism,

> *'We have found this man to be a troublemaker, stirring up riots among the Jews all over the world. He is a ringleader of the Nazarene sect and even tried to desecrate the temple; so we seized him.'*[14]

'Meshumod!' – 'Traitors'

When the Roman armies surrounded Jerusalem the Jews who had listened to the words of Jesus remembered He had warned of this event and so heeded His instructions,

> *'When you see Jerusalem surrounded by armies, you will know that its desolation is near. Then let those who are in Judea flee to the mountains, let those in the city get out, and let those in the country not enter the city. For this is the time of punishment in fulfilment of all that has been written. How dreadful it will be in those days for pregnant women and nursing mothers! There will be great distress in the land and wrath against this people. They will fall by the sword and will be taken as prisoners to all the nations. Jerusalem will be trampled on by Gentiles until the times of the Gentiles are fulfilled.'*[15]

A temporary lift in the Roman siege of Jerusalem made possible the escape of those who heeded the warning. The Jewish Christians recognised this opportunity and fled across the Jordan river seeking refuge in Pella. The siege of Jerusalem resumed during A.D. 68 and in the year 70 the Temple and Jerusalem were completely destroyed as Jesus had said they would be.

As a result of this action the Jewish community regarded the Jewish Christians as traitors, 'Meshumod', a term which is still used to describe Jewish Christians.

Life in Pella as described by Irenaeus, a distinguished church leader of the period, shows us the Jewish Christians continued their Jewishness,

> 'They practice circumcision, persevere in the observance of those customs which are enjoined by the Law, and are so Judaic in their mode of life that they even adore Jerusalem as if it were the house of God.'[16]

The Rift Widens

The destruction of the Temple and Jerusalem created a major disruption to Jewish national and religious life. The dispersed Jewish people were faced with the two-fold problem of how to retain their national identity and their religious obligations which were totally dependent upon the Temple. Jabneh was established as the administrative centre of religious life near the Mediterranean coast close to modern Tel Aviv. From this centre developed Rabbinical Judaism replacing Biblical Judaism and the priest was displaced by the rabbi as the leader of religious life which now centred entirely upon the synagogue.

The new form of Judaism was not acceptable to the Jewish Christians who saw Jesus of Nazareth as the Messiah fulfilling the Mosaic Law. Sealing their opposition to the Jewish Christians the authorities from Jabneh authorised the addition of an extra prayer to the daily prayers said in synagogues attempting to force the Christian Jews out,

> 'Let there be no hope for the apostates and let all the sectaries perish in a moment'

Yet the Jewish Christians continued to live among other Jews.

In 132 A.D. a nationalistic Jewish revolt under the leadership of Bar Cochba broke out against the Roman oppressor. Against their common enemy, (the Roman authorities,) the Jewish Christians joined ranks with the other Jews. Amidst this battle **the chief rabbi, Akiba, proclaimed Bar Cochba to be the Jewish Messiah. The Jewish Christians could not accept this declaration, and withdrew their support. They were denounced as heretics. Now they recognised that their hopes of convincing the Jews of Jesus' Messiahship were quite vain.** The contemporary historian Justin Martyr records that many Jewish Christians were put to death. This tragic act caused the complete separation of Christian Jews from the rest of the Jewish people.

We must understand the tragic situation of the Jewish Christians,

> 'There is no more tragic group in Christian history than these unhappy people. They, who might have been the bridge between the Jewish and the Gentile world, must have suffered intensely at the developments on both sides which they

were powerless to arrest. Rejected, first by the Church, in spite of their genuine belief in Jesus as the Messiah, and then by the Jews in spite of their loyalty to the Law, they ceased to be a factor of any importance in the development of either Christianity or Judaism.'[17]

Notes

1. *Matthew 27:25.*
2. *Luke 23:34.*
3. *Acts 4:27–28.*
4. *Revelation 13:8.*
5. *John 10:18.*
6. *Isaiah 53:5.*
7. Matthew 22:22.
8. Eusebius, *A History of the Church*, p.231.
9. Cross, F.L., *The Oxford Dictionary of the Christian Church*. pp.1089, 1131.
10. *Acts 10.*
11. *Acts 15:1.*
12. *Acts 21:20–25.*
13. *Acts 11:26.*
14. *Acts 24:5–6.*
15. *Luke 21:20–24.*
16. Schonfield, H.J., *The History of Jewish Christianity*, p.54.
17. Parkes, J., *The Conflict of the Church and the Synagogue*, p.92.

Recommended reading

1. *Hebrew Christianity*, A. Fruchtenbaum.
2. *The Jewish People and Jesus Christ*, J. Jocz.

7

The Deluded Church

'Fundamental to the mystery, too, is the truth that a Jew has to choose to be a pagan, while the gentile has to choose not to be.'[1]

Tragedy befell the Church when the truth of this statement faded into obscurity as the Church cut herself off from her Jewish roots and Bible truth. **The Church leaders not only failed to see that God had identified Himself with the Jewish people:**

> 'For the Lord has chosen Jacob to be his own, Israel to be his treasured possession.'[2]

But they failed to see that God had specifically said that His name would always be remembered in relationship with the Jewish people:

> 'God also said to Moses, "Say to the Israelites, 'The Lord, the God of your fathers – the God of Abraham, the God of Isaac and the God of Jacob – has sent me to you.' This is my name forever, the name by which I am to be remembered from generation to generation.'"[3]

The declaration of Bar Cochba as the Jewish Messiah was the watershed for the Jewish Christians separating them from Orthodox Judaism. In the same way the actions of Emperor Constantine of the fourth century separated the Jewish Christians from gentile Christians and the gentile church from Orthodox Judaism. The Jewish Christians, as we saw in *Acts 21:20*, continued to see that since Messiah Jesus fulfilled the Mosaic Law as a Jew it was both appropriate and imperative that they also retain their Jewishness.

Building on Sand

The 4th century was decisive in the history of both Judaism and Christianity. Teaching and decisions made by leaders of both

71

groups during this century had deeper and longer lasting effects upon the two groups than at any other period in their history. The Councils of Nicaea and Constantinople established the doctrines of the Church by steering their passage through various heresies and other pressures. At the same time the great Schools of Pumbeditha and Sura as well as the Patriarchate in Jerusalem were the centres of Jewish learning. Both Christianity and Judaism were active in seeking 'converts' and 'proselytes' which often brought them into direct confrontation.

Christianity was faced with the task of imposing moral and intellectual standards on the happy-go-lucky Roman world while Judaism was attempting to find a new basis for survival for its own community without either land, central authority or Temple. The Christian victory of official recognition – no longer were they a persecuted underground body – brought with it increasing power until it influenced the whole executive government of the empire. Where earlier the Church had called for equal rights with the Jews within the empire, now that she held power, in her intolerance, she denounced them.

Superficial Christianity was widespread among the upper classes of Roman society. This brought into the Church large membership which was probably already hostile towards the Jews. The Jews did not passively receive these Christian attacks, there were still outbreaks of turbulence, they still had people in official places, ready to rebel at any threat to their privileges. So fierce were some of these revolts that they required military force to suppress them. This was the environment of the Church Fathers.

Christianity's privileged position under Constantine enabled the Church to impose restrictive measures against the Jewish people by banning their observances. Circumcision became illegal, thus preventing conversions to Judaism and forcing Christians to forsake their Jewish heritage – at the threat of exile or property confiscation. Jews could no longer be sent money from the diaspora and were barred from holding public office. Even Sabbath observance was prohibited!

This dramatic change in the status of Christianity attracted many Jewish people away from synagogue life to the Church. This movement away from the synagogue was so significant that other Jews vented their anger upon these 'converts' in such harmful ways that within two years the severest of penalties were imposed upon offenders.

Jewish Christians Isolated

The Jewish Christians were rejected by both the Jewish people and the gentile Christians. They were accused both of wanting to restrict Christianity only to Jews and of wanting to impose Jewish customs on the Gentiles. This was not a new problem. It confronted the Apostle Paul.

The church, which was now becoming a growing power in the Roman Empire, required certain confessions from Jews desiring to convert. Prospective converts were required to renounce the Jewish people, their faith and observances and to vow not to be associated in any way with them. Some 'professions of faith' required the convert to confess damnation if he were to break his oath. In the words of one: 'May I be an anathema in the world to come, and may my soul be set down with satan and the devils.'*

The Jewish Christians held very dear the Jewishness of Jesus. They maintained that Jewish history was a total preparation for the coming of Jesus. The gospel had to be presented in its Jewishness to non-believing Jews if they were to believe in Jesus as Messiah. They also argued that Jewish believers could continue in their Jewishness and still be believers. The gentile Christians would not listen and concluded that the Jews were obstinately resisting Christianity. **The gentiles failed to understand what Paul had laboured to explain – that the fullness and completeness of the Jewish covenants of promise could only be found in Jesus the Messiah,**

> 'As ye have received Christ Jesus the Lord, so walk ye in him: Rooted and built up in him, and established in the faith, as ye have been taught, abounding therein with thanksgiving. Beware lest any man spoil you through philosophy and vain deceit, after the tradition of men, after the rudiments of the world and not after Christ. For in him dwelleth all the fulness of the Godhead bodily. And ye are complete in him, which is the head of all principality and power . . .'[4]

In their blindness the Church leaders failed to heed the warnings. The separation between the gentile Christians and the Jewish Christians caused misinterpretation of scripture, plunging the Church into grievous error.

---

* See Appendix 2.

Is the Church the New Israel?

Since Judaism was looking for a Messiah still to come, the Christians claimed that the Jews could only be expecting anti-Christ as Messiah.

Now came the great error. Since national Israel denied Jesus as their Messiah the Church claimed to be the true Israel! The Christian writers then proceeded to read back into the prophecies the 'Church' in place of 'Israel'. In reading the Bible this way the writers attributed the curses to natural Israel on the grounds of their disobedience. The blessings of God they kept for what they considered to be the true Israel, the Church, because she proclaimed Jesus as the Messiah. In abandoning the basic principle of scriptural exegesis, namely, noting who was speaking and whom he was addressing, and then interpreting scripture in that light – these early Church teachers lost sight of the truth.

The influence of this teaching is evident in the church even today. Although the Bible contains the warning not to add to, nor to subtract from it, we have Bibles published today with page headings continuing this anti-Jewish teaching. A King James Authorised Version with the following headings demonstrates the point:

(1) *Isaiah 9*, the prophecy of Jesus' birth and reign – 'the church's joy in Christ's birth and kingdom'.

(2) *Isaiah 30*, prophecy of God's blessing upon Israel and Jerusalem, is headed, 'God's mercies towards his church'.

(3) *Isaiah 44*, commences with words of comfort to Israel but is entitled, 'The church comforted'.

(4) In *Isaiah 45* God declares that He will raise up Cyrus to release Israel from exile, but it bears the inscription, 'God calleth Cyrus for his church's sake'.

(5) The Lord's Servant, Israel's redemption and restoration are foretold in *Isaiah 49* under the title 'Blessings of obedience. Christ sent to the Gentiles with gracious promises. Restoration of the church'.

(6) Then over *Isaiah 59*, concerned with the sinfulness and restoration of Israel, and chapter 60, foretelling the future glory of Israel, is written the title, 'The sins of the Jews.

Calamity is for sin. The glorious access of the Gentiles into the church'.

The seeds of anti-semitism were sown in the Church as these writers influenced Christian writers and theologians through the centuries. **This is 'the replacement theology' so much inferred and sometimes taught in churches today which simply states that the Church has replaced Israel in God's purposes. The result is a reluctance to accept the Biblical truth spoken by the prophets of God's unfailing covenant with Israel.**

We find the roots of this error reaching back into the third century. Eusebius, Bishop of Caesarea, provides us with very valuable information into the teaching of this period. He wrote two volumes: of the first volume of fifteen books, all are preserved, and of the second volume of twenty books, ten have been preserved. In volume one Eusebius claims to have proven that Christianity is both superior to and older than all other religions.

Eusebius' subtle distinction between 'Hebrews' and 'Jews' pinpoints for us the heart of the problem that continues to our own time.

According to him 'Hebrews' are the most ancient people in the world and their religion is the basis of Greek philosophy. They are neither Jew nor gentile. From the beginning they were 'Christians, and led a Christian way of life'. The Patriarchs lived lives pleasing to God and they lived as Christians not Jews. Abraham was a Christian not a Jew – according to Eusebius. Moses was a Christian who brought a special law for the Jews. That law was never intended for gentiles. Eusebius saw that the law was temporary, to be superseded by the new and superior law constantly referred to by the 'Hebrew' prophets. Eusebius uses many quotations from the prophets foretelling that the Jews will be abandoned by God as unable to receive salvation.

Eusebius presents the 'Jews' as of no importance and contrasts them with the older 'Hebrews' whom he says were the forefathers of Christianity. Hilary, Bishop of Poitiers' teaching of the Jews is summed up in his phrase that they were a 'people which has always persisted in iniquity, and out of its abundance of evil has gloried in wickedness'. Hilary and Eusebius presented to the pagan world a completely grotesque representation of the history of the Jews, preparing the scenario for the fourth century tragedy.

75

The Origin and Usage of The Word 'Jew'

Before going further we must understand the origin and development of the word 'Jew' so that we can see the abuse of the term by these early Church writers. Before the end of the New Testament period it had a perjorative use which these writers have perpetuated. We note 9 stages of development of the term **'Yehudi'** which has been translated 'Jew'.

(1) Originally 'Yehudi' applied to members of the tribe of Judah, the fourth son of the patriarch, Jacob.

(2) Its usage was then extended to include all those who dwelt in the area of the tribe of Judah.

(3) Later, during the seven years that David reigned in Hebron his territory was called the Kingdom of Judah (*2 Samuel* 5:5).

(4) During the period of the two Kingdoms (Judah and Israel) 'Judah' encompassed the territory of Benjamin as well (*1 Kings 12*:16–21). From then on 'Yehudi' applied to all residents of the southern kingdom irrespective of their tribe.

(5) After the destruction of Israel (the northern kingdom), the name 'Yehudi' was used more generally. For example in the book of *Esther* 2:5 and 5:13 we discover that Mordecai is of the tribe of Benjamin and also called a 'Yehudi'. After Haman's downfall many among the people of the land converted to Judaism – 'mityahadim' – *Esther* 8:17. At this time 'Yehudi' connoted a religious, political and national entity.

(6) The term 'Jew' has been mainly used by Jews and non-Jews outside the Land of Israel and in languages other than Hebrew. For example, Nehemiah, who was an official in the Persian court, refers to 'Jews' in his personal 'diary', and the book of Esther was most likely written by someone close to court circles and therefore out of the land of Israel.

(7) Hebrew-speaking Jews within the land were particular to call themselves 'Yisrael' which means 'Israel' (Israelites). It has been suggested that this was a deliberate reaction aimed at strengthening the identification with the nation's early history. For example, Ezra (in contrast to Nehemiah) uses the name 'Yisrael' throughout his writings.

(8)   From that period on the name 'Israel' is used in all Hebrew literature. The use of 'Jew' and 'Israel', as explained above, is evidenced in the gospels. Nicodemus, and later the Jews who mocked Jesus, called Him 'King of Israel'[5] while Pilate and the soldiers, who were Roman, called Him 'King of the Jews'.[6]

(9)   Gentile Christians in the early Church fused together 'Judaens' with Judas Iscariot who was regarded as the typical Jew. Since Judas was linked with the devil (*Luke* 22:3) there resulted the association of devil-Jew-Judas. From this developed the perjorative meaning of the word 'Jew' that has influenced Eusebius and others and which they have perpetuated. It is worthy of note that in the 19th century Jews began to call themselves 'Hebrews' and 'Israelites' to escape the problems associated with the name 'Jew'. The result was that very soon these new names took on the same perjorative association as 'Jew', as many 19th century novels testify.[7]

It did not stop there but continues right into our usage today. The Jewish scholar Pinchas Lapide undertook a study of explanations given for the term 'Jew' in modern English, American, Spanish, French and Italian dictionaries. He discovered the following: a usurer; a person who overcharges; person who earns money by unjust and sordid means; avaricious; 'Give the Jew a finger and he'll take the whole hand'; cheater; person of bad repute; sharp trader; satanic; to over-reach, referring to the proverbial keenness of Jewish traders; ruthless usurer; synonymous for obstinate miscreant; to cheat by sharp business practice . . .'[8]

'Usury' and 'Interest'

We now need to understand how these terms of moneylending and sharp trading came to be associated with the Jewish people who were formerly farmers and peasants. Since they were prevented from owning land and barred from the Christian industrial guilds they were reduced to work that Christians refused to do. 'Let no Jew exercise any trade or calling except . . . wherein no professional associations or guilds are found,' declares a Prussian law as recent as 1750.

Christians interpreted the commandment 'If thou lend money to any of my people that is poor that dwelleth with thee, thou

77

shalt not be hard upon them as an extortioner, nor oppress them with usuries' (*Exodus 22*:25), to prohibit them from lending money at interest to other Christians. The Jewish slaves who were the legal property of the Christian princes and popes were appointed as bankers, tax collectors and lenders. Interestingly, the Jewish interpretation of scripture came from *Deuteronomy 23*:19–20: 'Thou shalt not lend to thy brother money to usury . . .: But to the stranger.' They were licensed to make loans, rates of profit were fixed by decree, and a supply of coin was to be kept available when their owners required it. So the Jewish banker found himself with the distasteful task of collecting money, excluded from ordinary walks of life, and with work nobody else would do.

An extraordinary situation arose in England when Edward I expelled all English Jewry in 1290. With the disappearance of Jewish bankers Christians had to undertake their work. Since the Christians could not lend on 'usury' a new system was legalised. The banker was entitled to compensation from the borrower for the equivalent 'difference' in his wealth between the date of lending and the date of the money being returned. The amount of 'difference' was decided entirely by the lender, could not be paid back before the agreed date, and the 'difference' was often increased. The 'difference' system, in Latin 'quod interest', developed into the respectable system of 'interest' widely practiced by Christians. The injustices of the Christian practice led the people to protest in a popular medieval song:

'Give us back our Jews,
For the Jews were debonair
Greatly more, in this affair
Than now the Christians are.'[9]

This song reflects **the just and accurate work of the Jewish bankers who came to be internationally renowned for their expertise in handling money which Christians did not want to touch. Herein lies the paradox for it was this very issue that was to backlash upon them by those who propagated the idea of a Jewish conspiracy to control the world's finance.** But we must now return to the teaching of the Church Fathers who provided the theological environment from which this behaviour occurred.

Further Deception

Early in the third century the most important theologian of the Church, Hippolytus, so esteemed by the Church that he was later given the title 'saint', wrote not only blaming the Jewish people solely for the death of Jesus but claimed they constantly boasted of their part in His condemnation, suffering and death.

Another step in this breach with scripture was the gradual assimilation of the heroes of the Old Testament into Christian writings until they were presented as being associated with the past of the Church rather than being the ancestors of the Jews. The following is an example of the so-called Jewish view of ancient history as presented by the Church to her people,

> 'Moses they cursed because he proclaimed Christ, Dathan they loved because he did not proclaim Him; Aaron they rejected because he offered the image of Christ, Abiron they set up because he opposed Him; David they hated, because he sang of Christ, Saul they magnified, because he did not speak of Him; Samuel they cast out because he spoke of Christ; Cham (?Egypt) they served, because he said nothing of Christ; Jeremiah they stoned while he was hymning Christ, Ananias they loved while he was opposing Him; Isaiah they sawed asunder shouting His glories, Manasseh they glorified persecuting Him; John they slew revealing Christ, Zechariah they slaughtered loving Christ, Judas they loved betraying Him.'[10]

What a travesty of the love of God for man and especially for His elect people, the Jews, these scriptural distortions present. Their effect upon theology and Church teaching through the centuries has been such that God's love and purpose for the Jewish people has almost totally been unrecognised.

Poisoned Thinking

Anti-Jewish venom flowed with even greater freedom during the fourth century. **Since Constantine had checked the influence of Judaism, and Christianity received imperial favour, the Jewish people were no threat to the Church. Yet the venom persisted. This behaviour is an obvious indication of an obsession to persecute Jewish people.**

A significant preacher and writer of the time was Bishop John Chrysostom, who also was later recognised by the Church as a 'saint'. In a campaign to terrorise the Christians of Antioch against any contact with the Jews, he slandered the Jews in a most revolting way. Chrysostom delivered eight sermons covering more than one hundred pages of closely printed text, expressing intense hatred and malice to Jews, making accusations that were absolute lies:

> 'They sacrificed their sons and daughters to devils: they outraged nature and overthrew from their foundations the laws of relationship. They are become worse than the wild beasts, and for no reason at all, with their own hands they murder their own offspring, to worship the avenging devils who are the foes of our life . . .they are lustful, rapacious, greedy, perfidious bandits . . . inveterate murderers, destroyers, men possessed by the devil . . . debauchery, drunkenness have given them the manners of the pig and the lusty goat. They know only one thing, to satisfy their gullets, get drunk, to kill and maim one another.'[11]

Even worse, Bishop Ambrose of Milan organised the destruction of Jewish communities. In a letter of reply to Emperor Theodosius' demand for an enquiry into the riots, Ambrose wrote,

> 'I declare that I have set fire to the synagogue, or at least that those who did it acted under my orders, so that there would be no place where Christ is rejected . . . Moreover, the synagogue was in fact destroyed by the judgment of God.'[12]

Ambrose took it upon himself to sit in God's seat of judgment on the Jewish people. Both he and Chrysostom failed to realise that God had scattered the Jewish people[13], that they would be a blessing in the cities to which they were scattered[14], that God would regather them to their own land in His time[15], that God would judge the nations according to their treatment of the Jewish people in their midst[16] and that God would restore their spiritual inheritance and purify the land[17]. Even the Roman authorities were angered – the offenders were punished and the bishop required to rebuild the synagogue.

Cyril, the bishop of Alexandria, expelled all the Jews from that ancient and most important Jewish community of the whole Mediterranean region. All the other Church leaders – Tertullian, Origen and Irenaeus – although not as vociferous in their anti-Jewish stance, conformed to the policy of accusing the Jewish people of deicide and denying them any place in God's purposes.

To protect his new Christians against the influence of Judaism, Augustine portrayed the Jews as those who had been the sons of God and are now transformed into sons of satan. It has been said that Augustine's influence upon Christian teaching is second only to St Paul, but they are in head-on collision regarding the Jewish people. In his commentary on Psalm 18 he wrote,

> 'Of all nations the Jews were dispersed as witnessed of their own iniquity and of our fruit . . . thus our enemies serve us to disconcert other enemies.'

Had Augustine not read Paul's explanation of why the gentiles had been privileged with salvation? 'Because of their transgression, salvation has come to the Gentiles to make Israel envious.' Neither did he understand God's love for the Jewish people – *'As far as the gospel is concerned, they are enemies on your account; but as far as election is concerned, they are loved on account of the patriarchs, for God's gifts and his call are irrevocable.'*[18]

The Jews were now being connected with the fearsome figure of Anti-Christ. Many of the Church Fathers taught that Anti-Christ would be a Jew and that the Jews would be his most devoted followers.

Severed from their roots

The deluded teaching that flowed from the lips and pens of these influential men, denying the fulfilment of God's promises to the Jewish people not only resulted in unimaginable suffering for the Jewish people in the following centuries at the hands of the Church, but also resulted in God's judgment upon the Church, precisely fulfilling the Psalmist's warning:

> *'He who is pregnant with evil and conceives trouble gives birth to disillusionment. He who digs a hole and scoops it out falls into the pit he has made. The trouble he causes recoils on himself; his violence comes down on his own head.'*[19]

Collectively, these early Church teachers established a doctrine generally accepted in the Church and formulated into Church traditions by the early Church Councils. This led the Church along a path strewn with disaster and compromise with paganism thereby diverging from God's word and purpose.

At the Council of Nicea all the remaining ties linking the Church with the Jewish people were cut. The Council changed the dates of religious festivals moving their observance from the Jewish dates, which were in accordance with Biblical instructions, to observing them on dates of pagan festivals. Christians were admonished never to attend 'Jewish sacrileges'. This was a far cry from the practice of Paul who always made the synagogue his first preaching call in every town and city and only left the synagogue when all the Jewish community had heard the message of redemption in Jesus the Messiah. The Church was guilty of forsaking her first love and unless she repented as was required of the church at Ephesus [20] the judgment threatening the Ephesian church would befall her.

Severance from Jewish connections meant departure from Biblical observance both in doctrine, worship and behaviour. The resulting void was quickly filled with religious practices adopted from the pagan temples – luxurious buildings and furniture, ceremonious and ritualistic worship. Paganisation included praying for the dead, belief in 'purgatory' and the worship of saints and relics. Baptism and the eucharist lost their Biblical significance, again ignoring the stern warnings of Paul [21]. The struggles for influence and power among the bishops for superiority over each other and for secular power hastened Church decadence.

Jesus' rebuke to the Jewish leaders barely three centuries before now applied to the Church leaders, 'You nullify the word of God for the sake of your tradition.'[22]

The Church entered into a dark age for about 1,000 years after which God in His mercy began a process of restoration with the Reformation. The seeds sown in these centuries brought forth a bitter harvest. From this experience we learn the truth of God's covenant with Abraham.

'I will bless those who bless you, and whoever curses you I will curse.'[23]

Before leaving the fourth century let us remember that our study is concerned with the teaching and influence of the Church leaders. Generally, the relations between local Jewish and Christian communities were friendly. It was, in fact, these amicable relations that stimulated the wrath of the Church leaders, resulting in violent outbursts which sought to reproduce their own hatred for the Jewish people. Dr Lapide observes:

82

'Perhaps the greatest testimony to the complete falsity of the picture which the theologians painted from the second century onwards was that it took eight hundred years to be generally believed. Not until the eleventh century did ordinary Christians come at last to believe that the Jews were children of the devil, vowed to the destruction of Christendom, and to act upon that belief.'[24]

That God had not forsaken the Jewish people is apparent in many instances during these dark ages. One such instance highlights the blessing Jews were to Christians. In this angry outburst by Archbishop Agobard of 9th century Europe, we can see the purity of Jewish worship and teaching attracting Christians:

'Things have reached a stage where ignorant Christians claim that the Jews preach better than our priests . . . some Christians even celebrate the Sabbath with the Jews and violate the holy repose of Sunday . . . Many of the people, peasants, allow themselves to be plunged into such a sea of errors that they regard the Jews as the only people of God, and consider that they combine the observance of a pure religion and a truer faith than ours.'[25]

This is another example where Jewish people obeyed the words of their ancient prophet:

'Seek the peace and prosperity of the city to which I have carried you into exile. Pray to the Lord for it, because if it prospers, you too will prosper.'[26]

Notes

1. Littell, F.H., *The Crucifixion of the Jews*, p.63.
2. *Psalm 135*:4.
3. *Exodus 3*:15.
4. *Colossians 2*:6–10. A.V.
5. *John 1*:49, 12:13; *Mark 15*:32; *Matthew 27*:42.
6. *Matthew 27*:11, 29, 37; *Mark 15*:2, 9, 12, 18; *Luke 23*:3, 37, 38; *John 19*:19, 21.
7. Encyclopedia Judaica, Volume 10, pp.21–23.
8. Lapide, P.E., *The Last Three Popes and the Jews*, p.53.
9. ibid, p.55.
10. Pseudo Cyprian, *Adversus Judaeos*, as quoted by Parkes, J., in *The Conflict of the Church and the Synagogue*, pp.105–106.
11. *Chrysostom's Sermons* as quoted by, Parkes, J., ibid, pp.163–164.
12. *Eleventh Letter to Theodosius*, as quoted by Parkes, J., ibid, pp.166–167.
13. *Deuteronomy* chapters 28 to 30.
14. *Jeremiah 29*:7.

15. *Jeremiah* chapters *30* and *31*.
16. *Joel 3*:1–3.
17. *Zechariah 12*:10 to *13*:3.
18. *Romans 11*:28–29.
19. *Psalm 7*:14–16.
20. *Revelation 2*:4.
21. *1 Corinthians 11*:27, 29–30.
22. *Matthew 15*:6.
23. *Genesis 12*:3.
24. Lapide, P.E., *The Last Three Popes and the Jews*, pp.43–44.
25. Encyclopedia Judaica, vol.3, p.102.
26. *Jeremiah 29*:7.

8

'No Place to Rest and A Despairing Heart'

(Deuteronomy 28:65)

Conditioned by the years of the Church's perverted teaching, medieval man looked upon the Jewish population as descended from the devil for whom they were agents to destroy Christians and ultimately to rule the world. During this period Jews were almost wholly without legal rights. They were frequently massacred by the mob. In turn this encouraged the Jewish tendency to exclusiveness.

These long centuries of persecution led to Jewish alienation, and to their being compulsorily restricted to the most sordid trades. This, in its turn, filled the Jewish mind with bitterness towards the gentile world. **The Christian view of the Jewish people as satanic agents found its expression in the most hideous and horrific behaviour. One would not expect such from any human being – far less from Christians!** If this tragic situation had ceased with that dark age it would have still been too severe. But its influence reaches down through the Nazi Holocaust to our very own day!

Contrasted with man's deluded behaviour is God's faithfulness to His chosen people. As on a previous occasion in their history, so again He has faithfully protected and provided for them:

> '*He led you through the vast and dreadful desert, that thirsty and waterless land, with its venomous snakes and scorpions. He brought you water out of hard rock. He gave you manna to eat in the desert, something your fathers had never known, to humble and to test you so that in the end it might go well with you.*'[1]

The Unholy Wars

The Crusades, from the 11th till the 13th centuries demonstrated the horror of this perverted Christian teaching that claimed scriptural origin. Although designed as military expeditions undertaken by Christians to recover the Holy Land from Islam, and so to establish a Christian Kingdom based in Jerusalem, they were much more than this.

During the eleventh century Jews were expelled from many French and German towns. The motive was usually greed rather than a religious reason, as the seizure of Jewish property and commercial interests benefitted both the Church and the state. Much of this activity had its roots in the 'religious' zeal prompted by the call of Pope Urban II to the First Crusade in 1096. There began a pattern for all the crusades which obliterated complete Jewish communities throughout Europe en route to the Holy Land.

Attacks upon Jewish communities reflect again the utter distortion of scriptural teaching. In 1146 a Cistercian monk challenged the crusaders in the Rhineland to avenge themselves on 'those who had crucified Jesus' before setting out to fight the Muslims. A report tells of one Jew who was stabbed in five places in memory of the wounds suffered by Jesus.

After reaching and taking Jerusalem the Crusaders were let loose in the city where all the pressure from their long privations were released in an immense and terrible blood lust. The Muslim men, women and children were murdered on the Temple mount. The Jews were locked in their great synagogue and then burnt alive as the building was set on fire. The massacre was such that the blood of victims was knee deep. When there was no one else to kill, the victors went in procession through the streets of the city, still littered with corpses and stinking of death, to the Church of the Holy Sepulchre to give thanks to God for His blessing.[2]

Israel's God promised to avenge his people and to destroy their unrepentant oppressors:

'As for all my wicked neighbours who seize the inheritance I gave my people Israel, I will uproot them from their lands and I will uproot the house of Judah from among them. But after I uproot them, I will again have compassion and will bring each of them back to his own inheritance and his own country. And if they learn well the ways of my people and swear by my name, saying, "As surely as the Lord lives' – even as they once taught my people to swear by Baal – they will be established among my people. But if any nation does not listen, I will completely uproot and destroy it," declares the Lord.'[3]

Still trembling from the first Crusade the stirring of the second Crusade caused the Jewish people to cry out to the Lord, 'Alas, O Lord, behold, fifty years, like the years of a jubilee, have not passed by since our blood was spilt like water, because of the sanctification of Thy great, mighty and fearful Name in the day of the great slaughter. If Thou forsake us forever, what wilt Thou do for Thy great Name? Wilt Thou appoint misery a second time?'

And the Lord heard their cry and remembered His covenant and showed His loving-kindness to them. He sent **Bernard, the Abbot of Clairvaux**, one of the outstanding Church leaders of his century. Although Bernard was instrumental in encouraging support for the second Crusade, to release the Holy Land from oppressive Islamic domination, he spoke out with authority against the evil treatment of the Jews:

> 'Come, let us go up unto Zion, to the sepulchre of their Messiah; but take thou heed that thou speak to the Jews neither good nor bad; for whoever toucheth them, is like as if he had touched the apple of the eye of Jesus; for they are His flesh and bone;. . . for of them is said in the Psalms, "Slay them not, lest my people forget." '[4]

St Bernard refused to go with the tide of antisemitism. In exerting his great influence on the side of truth there was a turning of the tide of wrath away from the Jews. This was most particularly evident in Germany where Bernard's influence upon King Conrad not only changed the situation for the Jewish people but resulted in the king refusing to support the Crusade.

The Church's Fourth Lateran Council in 1215 undertook the most drastic curtailment of Jewish rights under the leadership of Pope Innocent III. There is an astonishing resemblance between the Anti-Jewish laws adopted by the Church at this Council and the Nuremburg laws of 1935 and the subsequent Nazi legislation. This Council made a law requiring every Jewish person to wear a distinguishing mark on their clothing – known as the 'law of the patch' – to further isolate them from the rest of the population. This was to become the forerunner of the infamous 'Yellow Star' of the Nazi regime, pinpointing the target of ruthless attacks and death. Medieval sculptures and paintings of biblical patriarchs and prophets wore the distinctive mark, while Jews of the day were often represented as having horns and a tail. Books of the day described a peculiar smell associated with a Jewish person, even though Jewish law required regular bathing not practised by non-Jews in the Middle Ages.

The Crusades have become a symbol to the Jewish people of the hostility between Christianity and Judaism. No longer was the difference a theological one. Rather, were Christians seen to be the implacable enemies of the Jewish people. In this environment the blood libel charges became widespread and, by the third crusade, the idea of a Jewish plot against the Christian world was well established. Jewish people who lost their lives in the crusades were venerated as martyrs for generations after, some even envied them, for they were a generation that had been tested and had proved their worth.

God's stern warning through Moses to His ancient people had become a stark reality in their lives,

> 'You will become a thing of horror and an object of scorn and ridicule to all the nations where the Lord will drive you.'[5]

A Spanish Inquisition

'Christian' Spain, in her zeal for maintaining purity of faith, used an Inquisitor during the 15th century to purge Christian heretics and Jews. Again, complete communities of Jews were wiped out, some 50,000 were forced to convert, while 300,000 fled the country. In less than twelve years 13,000 'conversos', Jews who had converted to Christianity, were sentenced to death because they continued to practice Judaism in secret.

The discovery of the many conversos who had remained true to Judaism showed that the segregation of the Jews and the limiting of their rights were not sufficient to suppress their influence. So, on March 31, 1492, an edict was signed expelling all the Jews of Spain, although it was not made known until 1 May. The exodus began. Around 100,000 Jewish people sought temporary refuge in Portugal. On July 31, the last Jew left Spain. Many Jews are known to have travelled with Columbus to the new world; among these were Jewish Christians of wealthy and influential families.

Lord Acton, the Catholic historian, made this pertinent statement regarding the Inquisition: 'The Popes were not only murderers in the great style, but they also made murder a legal basis of the Christian Church, and a condition for salvation.'[6]

The mass expulsion of the Jews from medieval Europe removed the greatest and the wealthiest Jews. In spite of Spain's acquisition of Jewish wealth, historians have dated Spain's economic decline to 1492!

This saga of Jewish anguish was another reminder of what God had declared would happen to the Jewish people when scattered among the nations:

> 'The alien who lives among you will rise above you higher and higher, but you will sink lower and lower . . . He will be the head, but you will be the tail.'[7]

But it also contained a testimony to His faithfulness to His covenant as we see in the lives of the Jews who escaped to the new world,

> 'Yet in spite of this, when they are in the land of their enemies, I will not reject them or abhor them so as to destroy them completely, breaking my covenant with them. I am the Lord their God. But for their sake I will remember the covenant with their ancestors whom I brought out of Egypt in the sight of the nations to be their God. I am the Lord.'[8]

As well as judgment upon the Spanish nation:

> 'I will bless those who bless you, and whoever curses you I will curse.'[9]

England Expels Jews

The Jewish population of England grew extensively under William the Conqueror in 1066. Their increased fortunes brought about their misfortune. 1144 saw the influence of the blood libel charges. In January, 1253, the Church became increasingly influential in the repressive measures against the Jews, in ordering that Jewish worship in the synagogues be inaudible to Christians. It also ruled that Jews could not employ Christian nurses or domestic help, Jews could not eat or buy meat during Lent, and no Jew could stop another Jew from becoming a Christian.

In 1280 Jews were ordered to listen to the conversion sermons of the Dominicans, and to refrain from building new synagogues. They were to wear an oblong white badge in the form of two tablets of stone, and to pay tithes to the Church.

Christians were not permitted to eat at Jewish tables or to be attended by Jewish doctors.

On July 18, 1290, the Jews were ordered to leave England before All Saints' Day. They could take with them only what they could carry while all other possessions went to the king. Altogether sixteen thousand Jews left England, cleared her of her Jewish population more completely than any other European country. Their exclusion from England was not ended until 1655 when Oliver Cromwell permitted their return.

A nineteenth century English historian wrote: 'If it could be said with strict precision of language that a nation can commit a crime, it would be true that one of the greatest national crimes ever committed, was committed in England when the Jews were expelled through the combined influence of the clergy, the traders and the Barons.'[10]

This tragic tearing of families from their homes, their land, their possessions, and even separation from kinsmen accords with the warnings of Moses,

> 'You will be pledged to be married to a woman, but another will take her and ravish her. You will build a house, but you will not live in it. You will plant a vineyard, but you will not even begin to enjoy its fruit. Your ox will be slaughtered before your eyes, but you will eat none of it . . . Your sons and daughters will be given to another nation, and you will wear out your eyes watching for them day after day, powerless to lift a hand. A people that you do not know will eat what your land and labour produce, and you will have nothing but cruel oppression all your days.'[11]

From a Polish Haven to a Polish Holocaust

The upheaval of 16th century European society forced the Jews to seek refuge elsewhere. Large numbers settled east, in the principal cities of Poland, particularly in Cracow, Lublin, and Warsaw. In peace their communities developed, they held responsible civic office, and their scholarship flourished. At a time when only the nobility and clergy could read or write, there was hardly one illiterate Jew.

A decadent Polish government unwittingly provided advantage for the Jewish population. An example was seen in 1643 when legislation was passed to suppress Jewish business interests. Profit margins were set: Christian merchants could make seven per cent profit while Jewish merchants were limited to three per cent! In effect, the population traded with Jewish merchants because their prices were cheaper and the Christian merchants were put out of business!!

Poland had a nomadic people – the Cossacks – who worked the land. Because of ill-treatment, the Cossacks rose in 1648 against the Polish gentry who owned the land. Jews and Jesuits were the administrators of the land. The Cossacks of the Greek Orthodox faith had long suffered persecution from the Jesuits. In the midst of the fierce battle between the Poles and the Cossacks lay the Jews who collected the taxes and acted as merchants. Protection from the Polish nobility ceased in 1648 when the Polish Army was destroyed; then followed wholesale death of the Jewish people by the Cossacks crying, 'Christ killers!'

After a respite of three years the Cossacks allied with the Czar of Russia and in 1654 massacres of Jewish people swept Poland. Catholic Poles annihilated the Jews in Posen, Kaliz, Piotrokov and Cracow, giving their synagogues to the Dominicans. By 1660, 500,000 Jews from 700 communities had been killed. The remainder of Polish Jewry has never been able to re-establish itself to its former strength even in pre-Second World War Poland.

No Room in Czarist Russia

The Church of Holy Russia had firmly etched in her memory the experience of the 15th and 16th centuries where nobles and even priests converted to Judaism. Russian policy was to keep the Jewish people out of Russia. Empress Elizabeth replied to a petition to allow Jews to immigrate to Russia: 'From the enemies of Christ I desire neither gain nor profit.'

One historian commenting on this attitude attributes it to the influence of the early Church's theology,

> 'Such pious royal disfavour can be traced to the very beginning of the Russian monarchy, and beyond that into the courts of Byzantium. The absolutism with which these policies were pursued derived its validation from the Greek Orthodox theology; and so deeply ingrained was this theology that every czar to sit on the throne of Holy Russia considered

91

it his sacred duty to protect the Russian people from Jewish economic interests, indeed even from the presence of Jews in their midst.'[12]

Taxes imposed on the Jewish population were double what Christians had to pay. In 1791 a law against them confined their communities to restricted provinces – the 'Pale of Settlement'. By 1808 this area was further restricted to ll provinces and laws forced Jewish people to change their occupation, language, dress and social habits! The country needed farmers and tillers of the land – the Jews were to do this!

Between 1640 and 1881 six hundred laws concerning Jews were enacted. Czar Nicholas 1 was aiming for one Russia, one language and one religion. He was determined to destroy Judaism as a distinct cultural entity. In 1827 he instituted a system of military conscription. This ensured that Jewish men became Russia's soldiers and imposed a law where a soldier's son became the property of the state. Children were taken from their homes and exiled into distant northern provinces for periods of up to twenty-five years. The aim was to have these children baptised. Those refusing rarely survived, and it is said 'over half' never reached the camps. As many Jewish communities could not provide their alloted number of children, children of the Pale were constantly kidnapped.

On 13 March, 1881, Czar Alexander II was assassinated. His son, Alexander III, began a course of autocracy. The Jewish people were blamed for the Czar's assassination, and he enforced a plan to solve the 'Jewish problem' in conjunction with his 'master planner' Konstantin Pobedonostsev, the head of the Russian Church. One half of the Jews would be baptised and one half would be starved to death.

Six weeks later dreadful pogroms began to sweep the land. In 160 towns and villages Jews were killed and their property destroyed. Priests and Russian peasants came to the defence of the terror-stricken Jews demonstrating it was the power of the Czar and not the people who were responsible for these measures against the Jewish people. In response to world protest at this carnage, the Russian government, to clear itself, said the pogroms were a result of the 'harmful consequences of the economic activity of the Jews on the Christian population.'

On May 3, 1882, new laws known as the 'May Rules' provided some protection for the Jewish people but also prohibited them from settling or buying new land in the Pale. They forced Jewish merchants to close on Sundays and Greek Orthodox holidays. These were followed by restrictions in education; later graduates were prevented from practising their profession. Large numbers of Jews sought refuge elsewhere. Many fled to America.

Beginnings of the Second Exodus

A Jewish doctor, **Leon Pinsker**, called for a second exodus. He wrote,

> 'Let us obtain dry bread by the sweat of our brow on the sacred soil of our ancestors.'[13]

Societies emerged all over Europe and in America stimulated by the vision. In 1882 three settlements were established in Palestine, populated by Rumanian and Russian exiles. Assisted by finance from Baron Edmond de Rothschild, others were able to follow. They were known as the BILU settlers. The name arose from the initial letters of the Hebrew phrase 'House of Jacob, come and let us go!'

God had promised not only discipline but also restoration,

> *'I will block her path with thornbushes; I will wall her in so that she cannot find her way. She will chase after her lovers but not catch them; she will look for them but not find them. Then she will say, "I will go back to my husband as at first, for then I was better off than now."* . . .
> *"In that day I will respond," declares the Lord . . .*
> *"I will plant her for myself in the land; I will show my love to the one I called 'Not my loved one.'"'*[14]

Czar Nicholas II's accession to the throne in 1894 put him in control of the largest Jewish population in the world – 6,000,000. He commenced to slaughter the Jewish population through an organisation of agents known as the 'Black Hundreds' with the cry 'Give them more blood'. The czar's repressive policies were forced on the whole Russian population – not only the Jews, and resulted in his murder in the revolution of 1917.

Blood Libel

The most cruel allegation against the Jewish people perpetrated by Christians, (with which, ironically, the early Church was charged) was the 'Blood Libel'. It was alleged that Jews murdered non-Jews, especially Christians, to obtain the blood for Passover or other rituals.

While blood sacrifice was practised by pagan religions it was prohibited by the Law of Moses. The origin of this accusation reaches back before the time of Jesus to the Greek ruler, Antiochus Epiphanes, and it has been suggested that the story was spread as propaganda to justify his desecration of the Temple.

The early church also suffered such allegations. The second century Church Father Tertullian complained:

> 'We are said to be the most criminal of men, on the score of our sacramental baby-killing and the baby-eating that goes with it.'[15]

Tertullian also describes the evil torture Christians suffered as a result of these accusations.

As Christianity spread through Western Europe, influencing the thinking and imagination, stories developed around the alleged inhumanity and sadism of the Jews. In Norwich, 1144, it was alleged that the Jews had,

> 'bought a Christian child before Easter and tortured him with all the tortures wherewith our Lord was tortured, and on Long Friday hanged him on a rood in hatred of our Lord.'[16]

This accusation of torturing and murdering Christian children in the form of Jesus' Passion continued in various forms throughout the 12th and 13th centuries.

We see the determination of the perpetrators of these allegations which were continued even after thorough investigations had proved them false. Emperor Frederick II of Hohenstaufen decided to clear up the matter concerning a particular allegation once and for all. He said he would have all the Jews of the empire killed if the accusation proved true, and he would publicly exonerate them if it proved false. To be sure that he would get the truth he commissioned 'decent and learned converts' from among the Jews of the West to undertake the investigation. The thorough investigation found absolutely no evidence to support the charges. **Frederick exonerated the Jews and Pope Innocent IV did likewise but little notice was taken of either the state leader or the Church leader.**

In the 19th century leaders of Jewish hatred used the blood libel as a weapon to arouse the uneducated masses in order to achieve their political goals. This was especially true in eastern Europe. The Nazis used the blood libel in full force for anti-Jewish propaganda. Russia had been the main perpetrator of the blood libel in modern times, particularly until the 1917 Revolution.

The British statesman, David Lloyd George, concisely summarised the illogical dilemma that besets the Jewish people scattered among the nations.

'Of all the bigotries that savage the human temper there is none so stupid as the anti-Semitic. It has no basis in reason; it is not rooted in faith; it aspires to no ideal; it is just one of those dank and unwholesome weeds that grow in the morass of racial hatred.

How utterly devoid of reason it is may be gathered from the fact that it is almost entirely confined to nations who worship Jewish prophets and apostles, revere the national literature of the Hebrews as the only inspired message delivered by the Deity to mankind and whose only hope of salvation rests on the precepts and promises of the great teachers of Judah.

Yet in the sight of these fanatics the Jews of today can do nothing right. If they are rich they are birds of prey. If they are poor they are vermin. If they are in favour of a war it is because they want to exploit the blood of feuds of the Gentiles to their own profit. If they are anxious for peace they are either instinctive cowards or traitors. If they give generously – and there are no more liberal givers than the Jews – they are doing it for some selfish purpose of their own. If they do not give – then what could one expect of a Jew but avarice? If labour is oppressed by great capital, the greed of the Jew is held responsible. If labour revolts against capital – as it did in Russia – the Jew is blamed for that also. If he lives in a strange land he must be persecuted and pogrommed out of it.

If he wants to go back to his own he must be prevented. Through the centuries in every land, whatever he does, or intends, or fails to do, he has been pursued by the echo of the brutal cry of the rabble of Jerusalem against the greatest of all Jews – "Crucify Him!"'[17]

Hear, O Israel

But the God of Israel who had the first word also has the last word. He will not be defied and He will triumph:

'The Lord called you a thriving olive tree with fruit beautiful in form. But with the roar of a mighty storm he will set it on fire, and its branches will be broken.'[18]

Paul explains simply how those broken olive branches are to be grafted in again so that the olive will thrive as never before:

'If some of the branches have been broken off, and you (gentiles), though a wild olive shoot, have been grafted in among the others and now share in the nourishing sap from the olive root, do not boast over those branches. If you do, consider this: You do not support the root, but the root supports you. You will say then, "Branches were broken off so that I could be grafted in." Granted. But they were broken off because of unbelief, and you stand by faith. Do not be arrogant, but be afraid. For if God did not spare the natural branches, he will not spare you either.

Consider therefore the kindness and sternness of God: sternness to those who fell, but kindness to you, provided that you continue in his kindness. Otherwise, you also will be cut off. And if they do not persist in unbelief, they will be grafted in, for God is able to graft them in again. After all, if you were cut out of an olive tree that is wild by nature, and contrary to nature were grafted into a cultivated olive tree, how much more readily will these, the natural branches, be grafted into their own olive tree!'[19]

We gentile Christians must understand two important lessons from this:

(a) **God is disciplining Israel among the nations. The nations are not given the right to discipline Israel.** God made this very clear in His statement through Zechariah:

> *'Thus says the Lord of hosts: I am jealous for Jerusalem and for Zion with a great jealousy. And I am very angry with the nations that are at ease; for while I was but a little displeased they helped forward the affliction and disaster.'*[20]

(b) **Paul warns us that we too will be disciplined by God if we are disobedient.**

The Psalmist reminds Israel of God's faithfulness to His people:

> *'He will not let your foot slip – he who watches over you will not slumber; indeed, he who watches over Israel will neither slumber*

96

nor sleep. The Lord watches over you – the Lord is your shade at your right hand; the sun will not harm you by day nor the moon by night. The Lord will keep you from all harm – he will watch over your life . . .'[21]

Then God encourages Israel with the assurance:

'"For a brief moment I abandoned you, but with deep compassion I will bring you back. In a surge of anger I hid my face from you for a moment, but with everlasting kindness I will have compassion on you," says the Lord your Redeemer.

"No weapon forged against you will prevail, and you will refute every tongue that accuses you. This is the heritage of the servants of the Lord, and this is their vindication from me," declares the Lord.'[22]

Notes

1. *Deuteronomy 8:15–16.*
2. Bridge, A., *The Crusades*, p.111.
3. *Jeremiah 12:14–17.*
4. Sparrow-Simpson, W.J., *Lectures on St Bernard of Clairvaux*, pp.172–174.
5. *Deuteronomy 28:37.*
6. Lapide, P.E., *The Last Three Popes and the Jews*, p.58.
7. *Deuteronomy 28:43–44.*
8. *Leviticus 26:44–45.*
9. *Genesis 12:1–3.*
10. Pike, L.O., 1873, as quoted by Lapide, P.E., *The Last Three Popes and the Jews*, p.55.
11. *Deuteronomy 28:30–33.*
12. Gade, R.E., *A Historical Survey of Anti-Semitism*, p.82.
13. ibid, p.89.
14. *Hosea 2:6–7, 21, 23.*
15. Encyclopedia Judaica, vol.4, p.1121.
16. ibid, p.1121.
17. Lloyd George, D., *Is it Peace?*, pp.246–247.
18. *Jeremiah 11:16.*
19. *Romans 11:17–24.*
20. *Zechariah 1:14–15.*
21. *Psalm 121:3–7.*
22. *Isaiah 54:7, 8, 17.*

Recommended reading

1. *A Historical Survey of Anti-Semitism*, R.E. Gade.
2. *A Distant Mirror*, B. Tuchman, chapter 5.
3. *The Crusades*, A. Bridge.

9

Preparing the way for the Holocaust

'The Holocaust was the work of Christians . . . and the fulfilment of Christianity.'

Such is the damning judgment of Yoram Shaftel, Israel defence attorney in the trial of John Demjanjuk (during March, 1987), who was accused of being 'Ivan the Terrible' of the infamous Treblinka death camp.[1]

A Mixture of Truth and Deception

Martin Luther, who received and declared the new truth of justification by faith not by works, also perpetuated an old lie. As a young man he was friendly to Jews and even fought against those who hated them. In 1523 in a pamphlet, 'Jesus was Born a Jew', he wrote.

'Our fools, the popes, bishops, sophists and monks, these coarse blockheads, dealt with the Jews in such a manner that any Christian would have preferred to be a Jew. Indeed had I been a Jew and had seen such idiots and dunderheads expound Christianity, I should rather have become a hog than a Christian . . . They were called names and had their belongings stolen. Yet they are blood-brothers and cousins of the Saviour. No other people have been singled out by God as they have; they have been entrusted with His Holy Word . . . I would advise and beg everybody to deal kindly with the Jews and to instruct them in the Scriptures; in such a case we could expect them to come over to us.'[2]

Luther's attitude was clearly in hope that pure Christianity would succeed in attracting the Jewish people. In later years, however, a bitter Luther completely reversed his opinion. Lashing out vehemently at the Jewish people, he wrote.

'The Jews deserve the most severe penalties. Their synagogues should be levelled, their homes destroyed, they should be exiled into tents like the gypsies. Their religious writings should be taken from them. The rabbis should be forbidden to continue teaching the Law. All professions should be closed to them. Only the hardest, coarsest work should be permitted them. Rich Jews should have their fortunes confiscated, and the money used to support Jews who are willing to be converted. If all these measures are unsuccessful, the Christian princes have the duty of driving the Jews from their lands as they would rabid dogs.'[3]

On 14 February, 1546, four days before his death, Luther preached his last sermon. His subject was the Jews, demanding that they be driven from all German lands. Ironically, **Luther's understanding of Paul's teaching of justification by faith was influenced by a commentary on Romans written by a 14th century Jewish Christian, Nicholas of Lyra.**[4]

Four centuries later a German historian wrote,

'It is difficult to understand the behaviour of most German Protestants in the first Nazi years unless one is aware of two things: their history and the influence of Martin Luther. The great founder of Protestantism was both a passionate anti-Semite and a ferocious believer in absolute obedience to political authority. He wanted Germany rid of the Jews . . . advice that was literally followed four centuries later by Hitler, Goering and Himmler . . . Luther employed a coarseness of language unequalled in German history until the Nazi time . . . In no country, with the exception of Czarist Russia, did the clergy become by tradition so completely servile to the political authority of the State.'[5]

In the early days of his career, Hitler cunningly used scripture and the Christian faith to win respectable support from the 'Christian' Germans. In a speech as early as 12 April, 1922, he had the audacity to say:

'In boundless love, as a Christian and a human being, I read the passage which tells us how the Lord at last rose in his might and seized the scourge to drive out of the Temple the brood of vipers and adders. How terrific was His fight against the Jewish poison; I realise more profoundly than ever before the fact that it was for this that He had to shed his blood upon the Cross.'[6]

Hitler's hatred for Jews permeates all his writing,

> 'I hated the mixture of races displayed in the capital, I hated the motley collection of Czechs, Poles, Hungarians, Ruthenians, Croats, etc, and above all, that ever-present fungoid growth – Jews, and again Jews.'[7]

Moses had declared to his people the horror of walking contrary to God's commands,

> *'All these curses will come upon you. They will pursue you and overtake you until you are destroyed, because you did not obey the Lord your God and observe the commands and decrees he gave you. They will be a sign and a wonder to you and your descendants forever. Because you did not serve the Lord your God joyfully and gladly in the time of prosperity. . .*
>
> *The Lord will bring a nation against you from far away, from the ends of the earth, like an eagle swooping down, a nation whose language you will not understand, a fierce-looking nation without respect for the old or pity for the young.'*[8]

And God constantly reminded His people of His faithfulness to them:

> *'I gave you my solemn oath and entered into a covenant with you, declares the sovereign Lord, and you became mine . . . This is what the Lord says – he who created you, O Jacob, he who formed you, O Israel: "Fear not, for I have redeemed you; I have called you by name; you are mine" . . . Listen to me, O house of Jacob, all you who remain of the house of Israel, you whom I have upheld since you were conceived, and have carried since your birth. Even to your old age and grey hairs I am he, I am he who will sustain you. I have made you and I will carry you; I will sustain you and I will rescue you . . . I say: My purpose will stand, and I will do all that I please . . . I will grant salvation to Zion, my splendour to Israel.'*[9]

The Protocols of the Learned Elders of Zion

Germany

During World War II the Nazi determination to destroy the Jewish people was 'justified' by some writings of an earlier time known as 'The Protocols of the Learned Elders of Zion'. These were widely distributed by the Third Reich and often quoted in their literature. It is important that we understand something of the background of these writings as they are still used and influential in creating anti-Jewish activity.

Before the rise to power of the Nazis the Protocols were most popular in Germany. These writings claimed the Jewish people exercised an occult power, and that they were determined enemies of German-Christian culture which well suited those in Germany who were looking for scapegoats for Germany's defeat. The Nazi Party used this theme right from its start.

Switzerland

A fact that is not well known is that the Jewish community of Switzerland, in Berne, 1934, took the distributors of the Protocols to trial. **The court clearly established that the Protocols were forged and therefore were not what they purported to be. This meant that the contents of the Protocols were false, they were malicious lies. But this did nothing to stop their misuse.**[10]

Let us now look at the history of the Protocols. During the Middle Ages many bizarre stories of Jewish behaviour were told by Christians. Often these arose from legends that the Jewish people were responsible for well-poisoning and plague-spreading. (We must notice that the Jewish people were often protected from some of these plagues because they lived by the Law of Moses, which incorporates sound standards of hygiene.) The next stage of this anti-Jewish plot was to say that there was a worldwide Jewish conspiracy determined to reduce the gentiles to slavery and even to exterminate them!

Spain

Later in Spain this thinking turned from a religious to a political emphasis. It spread to France where Catholic writers broadened the threat by linking Freemasons and Jews in an anti-Christian plot. In the late 19th century, the legend of the 'Elders of Zion' was written in Paris by an unknown author to encourage Czar Nicholas II to set up secret police against the Jews.

The unknown forger used an old French political pamphlet by Maurice Joly which had been originally written to expose the ambitions of Napoleon III. It mentioned nothing about Jews or Judaism. In rewriting them the author introduces a mythical conference of the leaders of world Jewry who, he claims, already had control of the policies of numerous European states and were not far from world domination.

Russia

Even Nicholas II, who was so dedicated to wiping out the Jewish population, recognised the Protocols were untrue. He noted in the margin of the manuscript given to him, 'one does not defend a worthy cause by vile means'.[11]

The wholesale slaughter during World War I which so dramatically changed the face of Europe, followed by the Russian Revolution in 1917, and the uprisings in Germany, caused people to look for a basic reason. The ground was fertile for the propagandists to suggest a 'Jewish Revolution' which was responsible for the pogroms in southern Russia between 1918 and 1920.

The Protocols were then spread in the West. **Many reputable newspapers raised questions on their authenticity and in 1921 a journalist, Philip Graves, pointed to the close similarity between the text of the Protocols and the pamphlet originally written by Joly. While this resulted in responsible people refusing to take them seriously they were nonetheless translated into all the main world languages and widely circulated.**

Egypt and Saudi Arabia

President Nasser of Egypt ensured they were distributed to all his troops. It has been reported that the protocols were, after the Koran, the most frequently cited book at the International Conference of Muslim Scholars gathered in Cairo in 1968. It is also reported that King Faisal of Saudi Arabia is presenting an attractively printed and bound copy of the protocols to each of his western visitors!

Malaysia

Dr Mahatir Mohammed, president of Malaysia, a persistent opponent of Israel speaks of 'Zionist plots' and 'international Jewish media'. He has said that 'the expulsion of the Jews from the Holy Land 2000 years ago and the Nazi oppression of the Jews have taught them nothing. If at all, it has transformed the Jews into the very monsters that they condemn in their propaganda. They have been apt pupils of Dr Goebbels.'[12] Malaysia has become a racist nation, patterning its actions literally after Nazi Germany.

Japan

Although Japan has a very small Jewish population, the influence of the protocols is becoming increasingly evident. Currently there is a spate of anti-Semitic books published in Hiroshima. The best-selling author, Masami Uno, argues that an 'international Jewish conspiracy' has created Japan's present economic troubles. He says Jews control major U.S. corporations and have engineered 'a targeted bashing of Japan'. He further asserts that mass killing of Jews by the Nazis during World War II is exaggerated.

It has been reported that two books – one entitled 'If You Understand the Jews, You Can Understand the World' – by Uno have sold at least 800,000 copies, thereby qualifying them as best-sellers. He claims that the bribery indictment of former Prime Minister Kakuei Tanaka in 1976 and the rise of South Korea as a competitor were part of the plot. The strengthened yen, Uno tells us, Jewish bankers have created to subvert and subjugate the Japanese economy. Other books that have also appeared on the Japanese market include 'Miracles of the Torah Which Control the World', 'Understanding the Protocols of the Elders of Zion' and 'Make Money with Stocks Targeted by the Jews'.[13]

We must recognise this subtle conspiracy for what it is. **This is not a conspiracy of Jewish origin against the world but the very reverse – a world conspiracy against the Jewish people!** Now that the Jewish people have the opportunity of living in their promised homeland, the life of the ghetto is past, but the conspiracy is now centred upon their homeland, Israel.

'Zionism is Racism'

The United Nations Assembly passed Resolution 3379 on November 10th, 1975, declaring **'that Zionism is a form of racism and racial discrimination'**. The significance and motive of this action is further highlighted by three points.

(1) November 10th, 1975 was the 37th anniversary of the horrific Nazi 'Kristallnacht' – 'the night of broken glass' – when Hitler's programme of genocide was launched against

the Jews of Europe. During that night in all the cities, towns, villages and hamlets throughout greater Germany hundreds of synagogues were set on fire, Jewish shops were looted, and Jews were beaten up in the streets.

(2) The Secretary-General of the United Nations at the time was the controversial Kurt Waldheim, now the premier of Austria.

(3) 72 nations voted in favour of the resolution while 35 nations voted against the resolution with 32 abstentions. Of those favouring the resolution only 14 were true democracies, 19 were communist and 22 were Muslim nations. It is encouraging to know that New Zealand, Australia, and Britain voted against the resolution. (See Figure 2).

The New York Times rightly put into perspective the situation which questions the faithfulness of the United Nations to its own charter: **'The unholy alliance of Communist and Arab Governments that pushed through the General Assembly in the odious resolution equating Zionism with "racism" was, in effect, challenging the very right to existence of Israel, a member state created by act of the United Nations itself. The original objective of the Arab bloc was to expel Israel forthwith.'**

This same fervour for the destruction of Israel is keenly reflected in the fiery speech of P.L.O. leader Yasser Arafat as he addressed the Palestinian National Council in Algiers on 20 April, 1987: 'We will continue the armed struggle . . . the Palestinian gun shall not be put aside until we reach Palestine . . . Our nation has determined that it will write its history in words of blood and fire, because the (Palestinian) soil is indivisible, and so is our will . . . I call upon our brethren in Iran to reach agreement (with Iraq) and to put an end to this war, so that all the guns may be directed to the liberation of Palestine from the clutches of Zionism and colonialism . . . We will continue to maintain fighting contact with the Israeli foe, until our revolution is victorious. We will fight, not just for the sake of fighting, but for the imposition of a just and comprehensive solution in our region, based on the legitimate rights of the Palestinian people – its right of return, of self-determination and the establishment of the Palestinian state with Jerusalem as its capital.'[14]

The Nation or Kingdom that will not serve you will perish (*Isaiah 60*:12)

While this book is centred upon the effect of the Church's extreme distortion of interpreting scripture, prejudicing the position of the Jewish people, it has been inevitable that our study recognise the effect upon the nations. We have seen God's judgment upon the Church for her rejection of the Jewish people. We must also realise that God has been judging nations and national leaders according to their treatment of the Jewish people.

History for many people is interpreted by secular historians who often see the events of history as a confusion of incidents, many of which do not relate together nor have any purpose. For the Christian who regards the Bible as the authoritative word of God, there is meaning, not simply that God is in control and all will work out well in the end, but definite direction according to the declared purpose and will of God. **Unless we have a clear understanding of God's purpose for Israel and the Jewish people, we need a new perspective of history,** which is more clearly stated as His Story. We will note eight important Biblical facts concerning Israel and the nations.

(1) The apostle Paul tells us that the hand of **God is controlling the nations of the earth and their boundaries in order that men may come to know Him:**

> *'From one man God made every nation of men, that they should inhabit the whole earth; and he determined the times set for them and the exact places where they should live. God did this so that men would seek him and perhaps reach out for him and find him, though he is not far away from each one of us.'*[15]

(2) Then Daniel tells us that **God controls the appointment of rulers over the nations:**

> *'The Most High God is sovereign over the kingdoms of men and sets over them anyone he wishes.'*[16]

(3) Jeremiah reveals to us that **God disciplines the nations using Israel as His instrument:**

On the Zionism Issue...
IT WAS DEMOCRACIES vs DICTATORSHIPS

An analysis of the political systems of the nations voting on the U.N. resolution to identify Zionism as a form of racism shows—

VOTING FOR THE RESOLUTION: 72 MEMBERS

Afghanistan	One-man rule
Albania	Communist dictatorship
Algeria	One-party
Bahrain	Sheikdom
Bangladesh	Martial-law dictatorship
Brazil	Military dictatorship
Bulgaria	Communist dictatorship
Burundi	Military dictatorship
Byelorussia	Soviet republic
Cambodia	Communist dictatorship
Cameroon	Parliamentary democracy
Cape Verde	Parliamentary democracy
Chad	Military dictatorship
China	Oman ....Absolute monarchy
Congo	Military dictatorship
Cuba	Communist dictatorship
Cyprus	Mixed rule
Czechoslovakia	Communist dictatorship
Dahomey	Military dictatorship
Egypt	One-party rule
Equatorial Guinea	One-party rule
Gambia	Parliamentary democracy
East Germany	Communist dictatorship
Grenada	Parliamentary democracy
Guinea	One-party rule
Guinea-Bissau	One-party rule
Guyana	Nominal democracy
Hungary	Communist dictatorship
India	Emergency one-woman rule
Indonesia	Military dictatorship
Iran	Absolute monarchy
Iraq	One-party rule
Jordan	Kingdom
Kuwait	Family dynasty
Laos	Communist dictatorship
Lebanon	Parliamentary democracy
Libya	Military dictatorship
Madagascar	Military dictatorship
Malaysia	Parliamentary democracy
Maldive Islands	Parliamentary democracy
Mali	Military dictatorship
Malta	Parliamentary democracy
Mauritania	One-party rule
Mexico	Parliamentary democracy
Mongolia	Communist dictatorship
Morocco	Kingdom
Mozambique	One-party rule
Niger	Military dictatorship
Nigeria	Military dictatorship
Pakistan	Nominal democracy
Poland	Communist dictatorship
Portugal	Military rule
Qatar	Sheikdom
Rwanda	Military dictatorship
Sao Tome e Principe	Parliamentary democracy
Saudi Arabia	Absolute monarchy
Senegal	Parliamentary democracy
Somalia	Military dictatorship
South Yemen	Leftist dictatorship
Soviet Union	Communist dictatorship
Sri Lanka	Parliamentary democracy
Sudan	Military dictatorship
Syria	One-party rule
Tanzania	One-party rule
Tunisia	Parliamentary democracy
Turkey	Parliamentary democracy
Uganda	Military dictatorship
Ukraine	Soviet republic
United Arab Emirates	Sheikdoms
Yemen	Military dictatorship
Yugoslavia	Communist dictatorship

Of the 72 members voting for the resolution, only 14 were true democracies. The other 58 were run by dictators, strong men or elite groups.

VOTING AGAINST THE RESOLUTION: 35 NATIONS

Among these nations, which included the U.S. and most nations of West Europe, were 27 democracies and only 8 countries run by dictators or strong men.

Democracies: Australia, Austria, Bahamas, Barbados, Belgium, Britain, Canada, Germany, Honduras, Iceland, Ireland, Israel, Italy, Liberia, Luxembourg, the Netherlands, New Zealand, Norway, Sweden, U.S.

Others: Central African Republic, Haiti, Ivory Coast, Malawi, Nicaragua, Panama, Swaziland, Uruguay.

Note: 32 countries abstained and 3 were "not present".

U.S. NEWS & WORLD REPORT. Nov. 24, 1975

A cartoonist's impression of the United Nations 'Zionism is Racism' resolution links the activity of the U.N. with that of Hitler and the Palestinian Liberation Organisation.

GG/A/59/Rev. 1
1 October 1947

GENERAL ASSEMBLY
SESSION 49

ROLL-CALL FORM

PLENARY MEETING 128   DATE Nov 29.

COMMITTEE _____ TIME _____

Question at issue ___ Palestine Partition ___

	YES	NO	ABSTAIN		YES	NO	ABSTAIN
AFGHANISTAN		X		LEBANON		X	
ARGENTINA			X	LIBERIA	X		
AUSTRALIA	X			LUXEMBOURG	X		
BELGIUM	X			MEXICO			X
BOLIVIA	X			NETHERLANDS	X		
BRAZIL	X			NEW ZEALAND	X		
BYELORUSSIAN S.S.R.	X			NICARAGUA	X		
CANADA	X			NORWAY	X		
CHILE			X	PAKISTAN		X	
CHINA			X	PANAMA	X		
COLOMBIA			X	PARAGUAY	X		
COSTA RICA	X			PERU	X		
CUBA		X		PHILIPPINES	X		
CZECHOSLOVAKIA	X			POLAND	X		
DENMARK	X			SAUDI ARABIA		X	
DOMINICAN REPUBLIC	X			SIAM			—
ECUADOR	X			SWEDEN	X		
EGYPT		X		SYRIA		X	
EL SALVADOR			X	TURKEY		X	
ETHIOPIA			X	UKRAINIAN S.S.R.	X		
FRANCE	X			UNION OF SOUTH AFRICA	X		
GREECE		X		UNION OF SOVIET SOCIALIST REPUBLICS	X		
GUATEMALA	X			UNITED KINGDOM			X
HAITI	X			U.S.A.	X		
HONDURAS			X	URUGUAY	X		
ICELAND	X			VENEZUELA	X		
INDIA		X		YEMEN		X	
IRAN		X		YUGOSLAVIA			X
IRAQ		X			33	13	10
TOTAL 1st Column:				TOTAL:			

The voting chart of the United Nations General Assembly on the partition of Palestine – November 29, 1947.

'You are my war club, my weapon for battle – with you I shatter nations, with you I destroy kingdoms, with you I shatter horse and rider, with you I shatter chariot and driver, with you I shatter man and woman, with you I shatter old man and youth . . . with you I shatter governors and officials.'[17]

Isaiah elaborates further upon God's use of Israel as an instrument of discipline, making four points:

(i)   God is sovereign – *'do not be dismayed, for I am your God. I will strengthen you.'*

(ii)   Israel will not be destroyed – *'those who rage against you will be as nothing at all.'*

(iii)   Israel is nothing in her own strength – *'Do not be afraid, O worm Jacob, O little Israel, for I myself will help you'.*

(iv)   Israel is to be used by God to discipline the nations – *'See, I will make you into a threshing sledge, new and sharp, with many teeth. You will thresh the mountains and crush them, and reduce the hills to chaff. You will winnow them, the wind will pick them up, and a gale will blow them away. But you will rejoice in the Lord and glory in the Holy One of Israel.'*[18]

The threshing sledge was a deadly instrument. The very sharp metal teeth under this heavy sledge slashed through and crushed the stalks and heads of wheat so that all was dust and only then could the wind separate the precious kernel of the wheat from the chaff.

(4) Micah reaffirms this function of Israel. The scenario is the nations gathered together against Israel but Micah makes the point that **the nations do not know their own danger in what they are doing** because they do not know God's purpose:

'But they (the nations) do not know the thoughts of the Lord; they do not understand his plan, he who gathers them like sheaves to the threshing floor.

Rise and thresh, O Daughter of Zion, for I will give you horns of iron; I will give you hoofs of bronze and you will break to pieces many nations.

You will devote their ill-gotten gains to the Lord, their wealth to the Lord of all the earth.'[19]

110

(5) Not only does judgment face those who harm the Jewish people but God even says that **He judges nations according to their treatment of the Jewish nation,**

> *'In those days and at that time, when I restore the fortunes of Judah and Jerusalem, I will gather all nations and bring them down to the valley of Jehoshaphat. There I will enter into judgment against them concerning my inheritance, my people Israel, for they scattered my people among the nations and divided up my land.'*[20]

(6) God also declares that **nations will come against Jerusalem and that they will suffer** as a result of their actions:

> *'I am going to make Jerusalem a cup that sends all the surrounding peoples reeling. Judah will be besieged as well as Jerusalem. On that day, when all the nations of the earth are gathered against her, I will make Jerusalem an immovable rock for all the nations. All who try to move it will injure themselves.'*[21]

(7) Zephaniah provides us with **an example of God's dreadfully severe judgment** upon Moab and Ammon because they have discredited the Jewish people and expanded their borders into the land allocated by God to the Jewish people – they are to be completely destroyed:

> *'I have heard the reproach of Moab, and the revilings of the children of Ammon, whereby they have reproached my people, and magnified themselves against their border. Therefore as I live, saith the Lord of hosts, the God of Israel, Surely Moab shall be as Sodom, and the children of Ammon as Gomorrah, even the breeding of nettles, and saltpits, and a perpetual desolation: the residue of my people shall spoil them, and the remnant of my people shall possess them. This shall they have for their pride, because they have reproached and magnified themselves against the people of the Lord of hosts.'*[22]

(8) **It was known among the nations that Israel was chosen by God and that judgment would fall on those who stood against the Jewish people.** This fact is made clear in the severity of the warning given to the gentile Haman, the Prime Minister of Persia, when he sought to destroy Mordecai, the Jew:

> *'Since Mordecai, before whom your downfall has started, is of Jewish origin, you cannot stand against him – you will surely come to ruin!'*[23]

Obviously it is God's ultimate purpose on earth that all men should come to know Him. His judgment is always balanced by His mercy. Persistent wrong has always drawn God's judgment in the hope that the wicked man will turn away from his wickedness and live righteously.[24] This is the reason why Paul wrote:

> *'I urge, then, first of all, that requests, prayers, intercession and thanksgiving be made for everyone – for kings and all those in authority, that we may live peaceful and quiet lives in all godliness and holiness. This is good, and pleases God our Saviour, who wants all men to be saved and to come to a knowledge of the truth.'*[25]

God expressed His purpose for the Jewish people:

> *'For as a belt is bound round a man's waist, so I bound the whole house of Israel and the whole house of Judah to me, declares the Lord, to be my people for my renown and praise and honour.'*[26]

I Will Enter into Judgment Against Them (*Joel 3:2*)

History has clearly demonstrated the truth of God's declaration to Israel,

> *'The nation or kingdom that will not serve you will perish; it will be utterly ruined.'*[27]

God is sovereign ruling the nations, using the nations to discipline Israel and using Israel to discipline the nations. He is a righteous and a just God, –

> *'I will have mercy on whom I have mercy, and I will have compassion on whom I have compassion.'*[28]

An example of His blessing and cursing, judgment and mercy, is seen in the message Samuel conveyed to the newly anointed King Saul of Israel,

> *'This is what the Lord Almighty says: "I will punish the Amalekites for what they did to Israel when they waylaid them as*

they came up from Egypt. Now go, attack the Amalekites and totally destroy everything that belongs to them . . ."

Then he said to the Kenites, "Go away, leave the Amalekites so that I do not destroy you along with them; for you showed kindness to all the Israelites when they came up out of Egypt."[29]

On another occasion God promised judgment upon the Babylonians for their destruction of Jerusalem,

'Before your eyes I will repay Babylon and all who live in Babylonia for all the wrong they have done in Zion,' declares the Lord.[30]

The archaeologists testify that this superpower was completely destroyed as the Lord had declared. There are many other scriptural examples of men removed from power and nations toppled as a result of their treatment of the Jewish nation.

Spain

Today's wide usage of the Spanish language, reaching from Spain to the Southern and Central Americas, accompanied by the many Spanish place names dotting the world, serve to remind us of the once-great Spanish Empire. An empire of great sea power, enormous wealth and renowned discoverers. An empire, like Babylon, that disappeared because of her treatment of the Jews.

Britain

Unlike Spain, Britain reversed her decision to expel the Jews but only after three and a half centuries of banishment were they permitted to re-settle in Britain. Not only was Britain given a second chance but she was given the privilege of administering the Jewish homeland prior to statehood.

In 1917 the British government (in the Balfour Declaration) viewed 'with favour the establishment in Palestine of a national home for the Jewish people' and promised to 'use their best endeavours to facilitate the achievement of this object . . .' Golda Meir states that the Chamberlain government's White Paper on Palestine (1939) 'gave way to Arab blackmail in much the same fashion that it was giving way to the Nazis'. The White Paper, in effect, ended the British mandate, although the death throes were to go on for another nine years . . . Today the answer seems incredible, even to me. The truth is that all that the yishuv (Jewish community) wanted from 1939 to 1945 was to take as many Jews as could be saved from the Nazis.'[31]

Britain broke her covenant with the Jewish nation and the Britannia who once ruled the waves, today possesses **nothing** of her empire.

Foreign Office,
November 2nd, 1917.

Dear Lord Rothschild,

    I have much pleasure in conveying to you, on behalf of His Majesty's Government, the following declaration of sympathy with Jewish Zionist aspirations which has been submitted to, and approved by, the Cabinet.

    "His Majesty's Government view with favour the establishment in Palestine of a national home for the Jewish people, and will use their best endeavours to facilitate the achievement of this object, it being clearly understood that nothing shall be done which may prejudice the civil and religious rights of existing non-Jewish communities in Palestine, or the rights and political status enjoyed by Jews in any other country".

    I should be grateful if you would bring this declaration to the knowledge of the Zionist Federation.

Figure 5. Letter from Lord Balfour, Foreign Secretary, to Baron Edmond de Rothschild, favouring the homeland for the Jewish people in Palestine.

Poland

Poland boasted of the largest European Jewish community and enjoyed the benefits which this former refugee people (the Jews) contributed to their magnificent country. But Poland's repeated massacring of the Jews has brought its own pall of oppression and destruction, leaving her a derelict nation. Poland's notorious ghettos of Warsaw and Lodz saw 3,000,000 Jews die in Auschwitz and other death camps. It was because of Poland's antisemitic reputation that Hitler was able to build most of his death camps there. Today it is not Warsaw or Lodz that is a concentration camp but the whole of Poland. While the Russian army controls Poland today, chief Soviet Communist Party officials enjoy the finest homes, food and service at the expense of the Poles who stand in long food lines for limited and outpriced food and wait for 15 years to get an apartment.

Germany

The superior German race who arrogantly sought to rule the world, is now divided by the same concrete walls, barbed wire and guard dogs they used to separate themselves from the Jewish people at Auschwitz, Dachau, Treblinka, Buchenwald, Ravensbruck, Bergen-Belsen. The Berlin Wall is a replica of the concentration camp fences the Germans built around the Jews.

Built in 1949 the 165 kilometre wall was to keep East Germans from fleeing communism. There are two 12 feet high parallel walls electrified to electrocute anyone touching them and 12,000 border guards. Between the fences are machine gun posts ready to shoot any trespasser, and vicious dogs running loose trained to kill. A visit to Dachau – the museum concentration camp – shows that the Russians have built the same wall around the Germans as the Germans built around the Jews!

When after 2.5 million East Germans had escaped to freedom in the West (that is nearly one out of every six people), during the night of Saturday 12 August, 1961, a 40,000-man special security and police force cut across streets, rail lines and tram tracks around the 1395 kilometre East-West border with barbed wire, trenches and concrete blocks. This was the night of the Wall. Berliners woke on Sunday morning to discover the two Germanys were separated – many family members were separated with no possibility of reunification. West Berlin which lies 180 kilometres inside East Germany is surrounded by the wall and is totally dependent on a few special air and surface access routes. It has been estimated that the Wall has cost $35 million.[32] There is a remarkable similarity between these events and the German treatment of the Jewish people from 1933 till 1945.

The Soviet Union

The Soviet Union's notorious anti-semitic behaviour is witnessed to the world today by the 300,000 Russian Jews who have been refused their right to emigrate to Israel. Not only has Russia prevented her 2.7 million Jews the freedom to travel but the nation has become a ghetto of fear where all Russians, except for a privileged few, are denied their rights to travel outside her borders. Russia sponsors the P.L.O. who train terrorists responsible for bombing civilians in Israel.

Syria has become a Soviet surrogate state enabling the Russians to stockpile offensive military equipment in Syria aimed at the destruction of Israel. Israel's entry into Lebanon in 1982 uncovered hundreds of tons of Russian-made weapons and ammunition hidden in miles of tunnels. All this revealed plans for a massive attack upon northern Israel which would have been a premature armageddon. God has declared His judgment upon Russia in *Ezekiel* chapters *38* and *39*. When Russia eventually strikes Israel upon her mountains, God will destroy the Russian military power.[33]

In His covenant with Abraham God had stated,

> '*I will bless those who bless you and I will curse those who curse you.*'[34]

History shows us that God means exactly what He says.

What you did not do for the least of these (*Matthew* 25:45)

The awesome precision of the fulfilment of God's warnings to the Jewish people is further witnessed as the nations met to discuss the solution to the Jewish problem. God had warned through Moses:

> '*The Lord will scatter you among all nations, from one end of the earth to the other . . . Among those nations you will find no*

116

repose, no resting place for the sole of your foot. There the Lord will give you an anxious mind, eyes weary with longing, and a despairing heart. You will live in constant suspense, filled with dread both night and day, never sure of your life.'[35]

At the same time **the nations stand warned about their responsibility in meeting the needs of the Jewish people.** Jesus presents us with a scene of the judgment of the nations.[36] The nature of each (whether a 'sheep' or a 'goat' nation) is decided according to how that nation has treated the people whom Jesus describes as 'brothers of mine'. Jesus' brothers are the Jewish people (see chapter 2) and judgment of the nations is according to their treatment of the Jewish people. This is in agreement with God's covenant with Abraham (*Genesis 12*:3), it is reaffirmed in Joel's prophecy of the judgment of the nations (*Joel 3*:2) and again in *Zechariah 2*:8.

An easy escape from our own guilt is to find someone else to be the scapegoat. While we so readily blame the Nazis for the Holocaust for which they were responsible, there was an opportunity for the nations to save the Jewish people from the Holocaust.

President Roosevelt organised a conference which met in July 1938 at Evian-les-Bains, France.[37] Only 15 weeks after Hitler annexed Austria the delegates from 32 nations met to decide on a method of rescuing the Jews of the 'Greater German Reich'. Also attending were officials of 39 refugee organisations including 20 Jewish organisations who had come prepared with photographs, reports and eyewitness accounts which provided an obvious picture of the doom facing the Jews of Europe. At that time the Jews could get out of Europe – that was not the problem. Where could the Jews go? Who would accommodate the Jews? That was the problem.

Two days before the Conference began Anne McCormick, a columnist for the New York Times, stressed its utter importance:

'It is heartbreaking to think of the queues of desperate human beings around our consulates in Vienna and other cities waiting in suspense for what happens at Evian. But the question they underline is not simply humanitarian. It is not a question of how many unemployed this country can safely add to its unemployed millions. It is a test of civilisation . . .

117

can America live with itself if it lets Germany get away with this policy of extermination, allows the fanaticism of one man to triumph over reason, refuses to take up this pledge of battle against barbarism?'[38]

The leading U.S. delegate, Myron Taylor, at the request of the American Jewish leaders, met with Sir Michael Palairet (the deputy head of the British delegation) to request that the head of the Jewish Agency for Palestine, Dr Chaim Weizmann, present the case for immigration to Palestine. Palestine had received more Jewish refugees than any other country. Sir Michael replied that his government 'would naturally prefer that this meeting should not take place.'[39] Taylor agreed not to speak with Weizmann before the conference.

The 39 representatives of the refugee organisations were allocated 10 minutes each to put their case, including the World Jewish Congress representing 7,000,000 Jews. The Jewish population of Germany at that time was only 350,000 and of Austria 222,000. If each of the 32 nations had accepted 17,875 Jews there would have been no Jews left for the Reich.

One by one the national representatives gave reasons why their nation could not accommodate Jewish refugees. Australia stated, 'As we have no real racial problem, we are not desirous of importing one'[40], – they accepted 15,000 over three years. New Zealand was unwilling to lift its restrictions. Sir John Shuckburg reported that the British colonial empire contained no territory suitable to the large-scale settlement of Jewish refugees – they received 9,000 Jewish children. Canada wanted only agricultural immigrants. The Dominican Republic accommodated 500. Only Holland and Denmark opened their doors to the Jewish people.

At the conference the delegation of Jews from Germany were refused the opportunity to speak but were restricted to written submissions. Golda Meir described the conference:

'I was there in the ludicrous capacity of the "Jewish observer from Palestine", not even seated with the delegates but with the audience, although the refugees under discussion were my own people, members of my own family, not just inconvenient numbers to be squeezed into official quotas, if at all possible. Sitting there in that magnificent hall, listening to the delegates of thirty-two countries rise, each in turn, to

118

explain how much they would have liked to take in substantial numbers of refugees and how unfortunate it was that they were not able to do so, was a terrible experience. I don't think that anyone who didn't live through it can understand what I felt at Evian – a mixture of sorrow, rage, frustration and horror. I wanted to get up and scream at them all, "Don't you know that these 'numbers' are human beings, people who may spend the rest of their lives in concentration camps, or wandering around the world like lepers, if you don't let them in?" Of course, I didn't know then that not concentration camps but death camps awaited the refugees whom no one wanted.'[41]

The bitter report of the Danziger Vorposten sums up the effect of the Conference: 'We see that one likes to pity the Jews as long as one can use this pity for a wicked agitation against Germany, but that no state is prepared to fight the cultural disgrace of central Europe by accepting a few thousand Jews. Thus the conference serves to justify Germany's policy against Jewry.'[42]

Hitler interpreted the refusal of the nations to do anything about the Jewish people as approval for him to implement his 'Final Solution'.

Rotten Roots (*Isaiah 5:24*)

We have seen how early Christian misinterpretation of the Bible quickly gave grounds to a world's hatred for the Jewish people. The same Christian misuse of scripture has established a teaching that has continued to influence Christian thinking and behaviour towards these ancient chosen people of God. This also influences the attitudes of both the Church, the nations and the world towards the State of Israel today.

Although today many people may not have heard of the Protocols of the Elders of Zion, this perverted teaching has influenced multitudes in their attitudes and behaviour towards the Jewish people. A combination of the teachings of Martin Luther and the anonymous writings of the Protocols prepared the mind of a complete nation to conceive and execute the most hideous plan ever devised by man – the Nazi effort to annihilate the Jews. The greater tragedy is that the Church remained silent!

Professor Rupp concluded a lecture on Luther by observing: 'As we follow Luther through the years, we find a signal instance of how we become like what we hate. We see a growing obstinacy, a hardening of heart, a withering of compassion, a proneness to contemptuous abuse – the very things he thought were the marks of judgment on the Jews.'[43] We have witnessed that this observation equally applies to many others through history.

Notes

1. *Hadashot*, Israeli daily newspaper, 20 March, 1987.
2. Gade, R.E., *A Historical Survey of Anti-Semitism*, p.51.
3. Barr, M., *The Unholy War*, p.121.
4. Gartenhaus, J., *Famous Hebrew Christians*, p.26 footnote.
5. Shirer, W.L., *The Rise and Fall of the Third Reich*, p.294.
6. *Christian Jewish Relations*, Vol.16, No 4, 1983, article *Hitler on Jesus*, pp.60–61.
7. Hitler, A., *My Struggle*, p.59.
8. *Deuteronomy* 28:45–47, 49–50.
9. *Ezekiel 16:8; Isaiah 43:1, Isaiah 46:3–4, 10, 13.*
10. Encyclopedia Judaica, vol.6, p.582.
11. ibid, p.582.
12. Foxman, A., *A Case of Racism* in *Australia/Israel Review*, Vol.12 No 8, 11–26 May 1987.
13. *Japan's Problem with Israel and Jews* in *The Washington Post*, 21 May, 1987.
14. *The Eternal P.L.O.* in *Australia/Israel Review*, Vol.12 No 8, 11–26 May, 1987.
15. *Acts 17:26–27.*
16. *Daniel 5:21.*
17. *Jeremiah 51:20–23.*
18. *Isaiah 41:15–16.*
19. *Micah 4:12–13.*
20. *Joel 3:1–2.*
21. *Zechariah 12:2–3.*
22. *Zephaniah 2:8–10 A.V.*
23. *Esther 6:13.*
24. *Ezekiel 18:21.*
25. *1 Timothy 2:1–4.*
26. *Jeremiah 13:11.*
27. *Isaiah 60:12.*
28. *Romans 9:15.*
29. *1 Samuel 15:2–3, 6.*
30. *Jeremiah 51:24.*
31. Meir, G., *My Life*, pp.152–153, 155–156.
32. Elliott, L., *Berlin: 25 Years of the Wall*, Reader's Digest, August, 1986, p.89.
33. *Ezekiel* chapters 38 and 39.
34. *Genesis 12:3.*
35. *Deuteronomy 28:64–66.*
36. *Matthew 25:31–46.*

37. Laffin, J., *The Israeli Mind*, p.231.
38. Morse, A.D., *While Six Million Died*, p.210.
39. ibid, p.211.
40. ibid, p.212.
41. Meir, G., *My Life*, pp.151–152.
42. Morse, A.D., *While Six Million Died*, p.214.
43. Rupp, E.G., *Martin Luther and the Jews*, p.22.

10

'I will bless those who bless you'

'The crucifixion and the resurrection of the Jewish people is a sign that God is not mocked, that pride brings the biggest battalions low in the end, that the Author and Judge of history blesses the Suffering Servant and brings the human hero low. Do the baptised believe these truths, or must they be numbered among the blind and deaf when the Messiah comes?'[1]

Peter Abelard was one of 'the baptised' who not only believed these truths but stood up early in the 12th century with the Jewish people against a background of severe Jewish persecution. At first he was denounced by the notable monks of Clairvaux, then by other church authorities and finally by Pope Innocent II.

Abelard's courageous stand, like that of Bernard of Clairvaux reminds us that **all through these dark centuries of anti-Jewish activity there were strong men of God – Church dignitaries and ordinary Christians – who stood out against the tide of wicked teaching and its subsequent infamous action against the Jewish people.**

Jacob shall return . . . the puritan's teaching

A turning of the tide was evidenced during the 17th century, particularly in England. The Puritans, who upheld Bible truth and authority, widely influenced public thinking and attitude in England and Holland. A vital concern for the Jewish people was born, and although not all Puritan aspirations were accomplished during their period, the Jews were readmitted to England. We can trace from the Puritan influence some action that later blossomed into the restored Jewish homeland.

In January, 1649, Ebenezer and Joanna Cartwright, English Puritans living in Amsterdam, petitioned the English government:

'That this Nation of England, with the inhabitants of the Netherlands, shall be the first and the readiest to transport Israel's sons and daughters in their ships to the Land promised to their forefathers, Abraham, Isaac and Jacob for an everlasting Inheritance.'[2]

The petitioners were not only moved to see the Jewish homeland restored but also expressed concern for the return of Jewish people to England. The petition continued, that the Jews 'may again be received and permitted to trade and dwell amongst you in this Land'. After 350 years' banishment from English shores this petition – 'Petition of the Jews for Repealing the Act of Parliament for their Banishment out of England' – was part of the process that reversed this decision. **The petition also reflects the power of the Bible upon people's attitudes and action in a nation.**

In returning to the Bible, the Puritans gave much attention to the Old Testament, emphasising Hebraism in the family and community life. The names of the heroes and patriarchs were conferred upon their children at baptism. Sunday observance was coloured by the ancient Sabbath. Their conduct was based upon the life style and principles of the faithful as recorded in the books of the Judges and Kings.

Accordingly, priority was given to the Hebrew language even above Greek, the New Testament language. The three 'Biblical languages', Hebrew, Greek and Latin, were taught to children and were a prerequisite to theological study – the main attraction at the universities. Biblical scholarship and exegesis dominated the intellectual activity of the age. Interest in the Jewish people was not confined to the scholars but touched the people through books, treatises, lectures and sermons – it was widespread.

In December 1655 Cromwell, the Protector of England, convened a special committee of judges, clergy and merchants to consider re-opening the doors for Jewish people to return to England. The statement of the clergy acknowledges the unique responsibility they believed England had towards the Jewish people – 'The good people of England did generally more believe the promises of the calling of the Jews and more correctly pray for it than any other nation,' and that in admitting them may bring about this 'calling'. They believed this instance provided England with an opportunity to repent of her sins towards the Jewish people – 'We are children of the same Father

Abraham, they naturally after the flesh, we believers after the Spirit.'[3]

England permitted the re-entry of Jews. But we need to notice what really motivated Puritan interest in the Jewish people being restored to England and why they should have been restored to the Promised Land. Puritans believed that Jesus was to reign for a millennium in Jerusalem and that prior to His return to earth, the Jewish people would have to be restored to their land. Permitting their re-admission to England could have facilitated their 'conversion', fulfilling a Biblical requirement for Jesus' return.

Some historians argue that England's readmission of the Jews was dictated by the aid the Jewish community could have contributed in the war with Spain. That may have been a factor at the time, but it is obvious that **it was the teaching of the Puritans and the power of biblical conviction that changed the English heart convincing her to make right her wrongs to the Jewish people.**

Jerusalem shall be inhabited

The Puritan fire was quenched as the age of reason undermined the authority of scripture during the 18th century. No longer could the Bible be interpreted – certainly by the Christians of that day – to convey the hope of the Lord's return, since prophecy was 'irrational', and so any thought of a Jewish homeland was dropped.

Although Puritans were ejected from the Established Church, excluded from membership in institutions of learning and deprived of civil rights until 1689, they persisted in keeping alive their tradition until a better season. The season was the 19th century and the harvest was the Evangelical Revival.

Emphasis upon the Old Testament was renewed as the authority of the Bible was restored. Stimulated by the prophecies of Jerusalem's restoration and the return of the Jewish people to their ancient land Christians felt bound to assist this restoration process.

A characteristic of the Evangelical Revival was the birth of many gospel societies including the British and Foreign Bible Society, the Religious Tract Society, the Church Missionary Society and the London Society for Promoting Christianity among the Jews. For a long time the last of these, known as the

Jews' Society, was the most popular of all the missionary societies.

At the Jews' Society meetings, sermons presented Jesus as the Jewish Messiah. The Jews' Chapel was established with free education for Jewish children. Christian support for the work was phenomenal. After five years the society had the support of 2,000 contributors. Records show that by 1841 both the Archbishops of Canterbury and York along with 23 bishops, many priests and noble gentry, were among the patrons. By 1850 the society, later known as the Church's Ministry amongst the Jews (C.M.J.), had 78 missionaries serving in 32 branch offices scattered from London to Jerusalem.

Britain's early influence on Jewish Restoration

A driving force in this movement was **Anthony Ashley Cooper, the seventh Earl of Shaftsbury.** As an evangelical Christian, Ashley's deep concerns were for improving the morals, working conditions, and general standard of life in Britain. He was highly motivated by his belief in the nearness of the return of Jesus which 'has always been a moving principle in my life for I see everything going on in the world subordinate to this great event.'[4] The return of the Jewish people to their own land he knew to be a requirement before Jesus could return. From the inscription on the ring worn on his right hand, his heart-concern was obvious: 'Oh, pray for the peace of Jerusalem!' One can almost hear the echo of the Psalmist voice – 'If I forget you, O Jerusalem, let my right hand wither! Let my tongue cleave to the roof of my mouth, if I do not remember you, if I do not set Jerusalem above my highest joy!'[5]

Ashley, a leader of the Jews' Society, envisaged an Anglican bishopric in Jerusalem, believing that a transplant of the work in England on to the soil of Palestine would lead to the restoration of the Jewish homeland. The extent of his enthusiasm to this end is seen in his writing when **Britain appointed the first vice-consul of any nation to Jerusalem:**

'Took leave this morning of Young, who has just been appointed Her Majesty's Vice-Consul at Jerusalem! What a wonderful event it is! **The ancient city of the people of God is about to resume a place among the nations, and England**

is the first of Gentile kingdoms that ceases "to tread her down." [6]

Ashley liberally shared his views with politician friends and used opportunities whenever they arose to win support for the Jewish cause. Following the publication of the first of many books on travel in the Holy Land, he reviewed the book to publicise his dream of a restored Jewish homeland under the care of the Anglican Church.

He used as evidence for the urgent fulfilment of his dream, a letter received from Poland describing increasing persecution which was creating a resurgence of desire among the Jews of Russia and Poland to return to their ancient homeland. Enthusiastically, Ashley described the Jews' Society's plan to build an Anglican Church in Jerusalem, preferably on Mt Zion. He explained that already missionaries were holding the first ever protestant services in Hebrew for the small congregation of proselytes 'on the Mount of the Holy City itself in the language of the prophets and in the spirit of the Apostles.' His words mirror his satisfaction from the occasion as 'one of the most striking that have occurred in modern days, perhaps in any days since the corruptions began in the Church of Christ.' [7]

While Ashley's motivation for this Jewish homeland was scriptural, he had also surveyed practical requirements. He noted that Palestine was suited to agriculture and foresaw that it would be ideal for producing cotton, silk and olive oil, thereby creating employment as well as trade appropriate to England's needs. He also saw that the 'recall of the Jews to their ancient homeland' could become a stabilising influence in the shaky Muslim-controlled Ottoman Empire. It is important to note that Ashley made no suggestion of developing an independent Jewish state, and that all this activity was taking place twenty years **before** the birth of Theodore Herzl.

First Bishop to Jerusalem

Although a change of government prevented any further action towards a Jewish homeland, the Church of England created a bishopric in Jerusalem and consecrated a former Jewish rabbi as its first bishop, **Michael Solomon Alexander,** who had been professor of Hebrew and Arabic at King's College. This event was the greatest achievement of the Jews' Society and was seen by that Society as a sign for the restoration of the ancient kingdom of Israel as a Church of England diocese.

On Sunday November 7, 1841, in Lambeth Palace, Alexander was consecrated Bishop of Jerusalem by the Archbishop of Canterbury and the bishops of London, Rochester and New Zealand in the presence of a distinguished company. Working among the Jewish people proved laborious, reaping a small harvest, and taking its heavy toll upon his strength. Within five years he was dead. The weight of the task was summed up in the words of one Jewish observer, 'the hill of Zion is not a likely place for a Jew to forsake the faith of his fathers.'

The Puritans had motivated the British to re-admit the Jewish people to England and sowed the seed of a Jewish homeland. The Evangelicals, and especially the seventh Earl of Shaftsbury, pursued the vision of a Jewish homeland until definite steps were made in establishing that homeland.

Although the Evangelical enthusiasm for the Jewish people and their homeland waned, and the Jewish people refused to be inspired by a move from their comfortable homes to endure the hardships of settling and developing their ancient homeland, the interest was taken up from a very different direction. At first for imperial reasons, but then by Christians looking backwards into history to understand the Jewish roots of their faith, rather than to see themselves fulfilling prophecy or looking for the return of Jesus.

Britain's part in spying out the land

Benjamin Disraeli's rise to prominence in politics, and onward to serve as Britain's prime minister at the zenith of her imperial power, certainly demonstrated the English heart change towards Jewish people. This Jewish man, who identified with the Christian faith, precisely defined the Christian debt and responsibility to the Jewish people in his speech on Jewish Emancipation in the House of Commons:

'Where is your Christianity if you do not believe in their Judaism? On every altar . . . we find the table of Jewish law . . . All the early Christians were Jews . . . every man in the early ages of the Church by whose power or zeal or genius the Christian faith was propagated, was a Jew . . . If you had not forgotten what you owe to this people . . . you as Christians would be only too ready to seize the first opportunity of meeting the claims of those who profess this religion.'[8]

Disraeli's distinction was that of an empire builder who had no association with Ashley, nor was he a Jewish nationalist. His part in securing the Jewish homeland under British control was primarily concerned with Britain's interests abroad. As Britain's empire expanded eastward in the later 19th century, he acquired for Britain the Suez Canal, a vital link with India and the developing extremities of her empire. Simply, Suez had to be guarded and Palestine's close proximity provided an excellent guard-post for the British.

Rationalism replaced Evangelicalism in the unfolding drama of the Jewish return to their homeland. Rationalist Christians were determined to prove the Bible as history in contrast to the Evangelicals who needed no proof of the Bible's accuracy or historicity but looked forward to prophetic fulfilment.

This was an age of scientific discovery and the questioning of a myriad of previously held facts. Human history was born in the Holy Land. Jewish roots were therefore the roots of mankind and certainly the roots of Christianity – they had to be investigated. One man wrote about the Jewish prophets: 'they taught men the true nature of God, that he was a God of love as well as of justice, the Father as well as the judge of mankind.'[9] The task they set themselves was to recover the authentic past and discover the real people of the Bible, which was accomplished through the fields of archaeology, topography, meteorology, botany, zoology.

Even the War Office was caught up in this interest in the Holy Land. Engineers were sent out on a task never before undertaken – surveying and mapping the Holy Land! They set out to discover the sites of ancient cities, they identified tribal boundaries, discovered important markers and boundary stones, and uncovered ancient highways. The dead unknown past came alive! Former scepticism that this was once fertile land 'flowing with milk and honey' was not only totally disproved by their discoveries, but it was realised that this once highly productive land required only cultivation to restore its fertility.

If the Puritans and Evangelicals had widely disseminated the idea of a Jewish homeland and stimulated action towards this end, the Rationalists measured the land, observed its

nature, and investigated its potential. The ancient Jewish homeland had the potential to support a large population, was the verdict. The British now knew Palestine thoroughly and were equipped and prepared to defend it.

A Jewish Homeland at last!

Even if she desired to, Britain was not in a position to give the land to the Jewish people as a homeland, since Palestine was not among her possessions. Long ago she realised the danger of a world ruler dominating Europe and controlling the Middle East. Protection from Cairo to Constantinople was vital to maintain, plus free access to the Far East. Therefore she diligently patrolled the Mediterranean. In order to maintain that balance she had consistently supported the crumbling Turkish Empire against pressures from Russia, France, Prussia and Germany, believing that the disappearance of the old Turkish Empire would drastically change the face of the Middle East.

We can now see why the British War Office was so actively involved in measuring the ancient Jewish homeland. Britain had prepared herself thoroughly for that day when the Turkish Empire fell. Disraeli's securing of the Suez Canal and Cyprus had not only been strategic then, but proved even more so when the storm clouds burst forth in World War I. The Islamic Turkish Empire, which had dominated the Middle East for 400 years at last crumbled.

The scene was set for a man of conviction to lead favourably disposed leaders to proclaim this as the Jewish homeland. **Arthur Balfour** was that man. Formerly Britain's Prime Minister, now Foreign Secretary, Lord Balfour wrote to Baron Edward de Rothschild as the representative of the Jewish people, on 2 November, 1917:

> **'His Majesty's Government view with favour the establishment in Palestine of a national home for the Jewish people, and will use their best endeavours to facilitate the achievement of this object, it being clearly understood that nothing shall be done which may prejudice the civil and religious rights of existing and non-Jewish communities in Palestine, or the rights and political status enjoyed by Jews in any other country.'**[10]

Balfour had been schooled in the Bible since childhood, the characters and places of the Bible being very real to him. Unlike the Puritans and Evangelicals he was not a religious enthusiast, nevertheless he was very interested in the 'people of the Book'. Unlike other Christian Englishmen who assisted the restoration of the Jewish people to their land, Balfour's concern was for **the Jews as people to whom Christians owed an 'immeasurable debt'** – which could in part be paid by returning them to their homeland. He was in no way motivated by any biblical interpretation of a millennium, nor by imperialist gains. He wrote, 'that the position of the Jew is unique. **For them race, religion and country are inter-related as they are inter-related in the case of no other religion and no other country on earth.'**[11]

We cannot pass on before we recognise the remarkable contribution made by a Jewish scientist to the war effort in Britain. Although the Allies were marching to victory, Britain was desperately short of gun powder to arm her navy. Winston Churchill, First Lord of the Admiralty, approached a brilliant Jewish chemist, **Chaim Weizmann** who in turn produced 30,000 tons of synthetic acetone that was used in the manufacture of cordite gun powder. Dr Weizmann was asked how the British Government might reward his services. He replied, 'There is only one thing I want . . . a national homeland for my people.' The Balfour Declaration was Britain's response. Again we are reminded of God's covenant with Abraham:

> '*Abraham will surely become a great and powerful nation, and all nations on earth will be blessed through him.*'[12]

General **Edmund Allenby**, a devout Christian, and commander of the allied forces in Palestine, received from the Turkish authorities the keys of Jerusalem on 11 December, 1917. During 1918 he completed the conquest of the old Empire, succeeding where the Crusaders had failed, to bring the whole of this territory under 'Christian' rule for the first time in history. From that time Britain assumed responsibility for the area until 1922 when the League of Nations officially conferred upon her the Palestine Mandate.

Although several significant Christian contributions towards the rebirth of Israel could be mentioned, we will only refer to one – the very practical contribution of a committed Christian whose influence is even today evident in Israel: **Orde Wingate**. It is impossible for us to understand his motivation unless we know something of his faith. Soon after Wingate's arrival he

131

explained to a Jewish military commander that his sympathies were with Zionism and that 'there is only one important book on the subject, the Bible, and I have read it thoroughly.' He continued:

'This is the cause of your survival. I count it as my privilege to help you fight your battle. To that purpose I want to devote my life. I believe that the very existence of mankind is justified when it is based on the moral foundation of the Bible. Whoever dares lift a hand against you and your enterprise here should be fought against. Whether it is jealousy, ignorance or perverted doctrine such as have made your neighbours rise against you, or "politics" which make some of my countrymen support them, I shall fight with you against any of these influences. But remember that it is your battle. My part, which I say I feel to be a privilege, is only to help you.'[13]

Captain Wingate was posted as an intelligence officer to a most unsettled Jerusalem in 1936. Since the Arab riots of 1929 the peaceful atmosphere was never regained, but both the British and Jewish policy remained one of defence. Coinciding with Wingate's arrival, a new wave of Arab terror broke out where guerillas destroyed homes, towns, and agricultural settlements in the most savage outbursts. It was clear to this young officer that there were three factions in this land – the Arabs, the Jews, and the British Administration who failed to keep their agreement.

Wingate trained special units of men (known as the Special Night Squads) in unusual techniques that proved extremely successful in defence from the marauding Arab attacks. In contrast to the official defence policy employed, where many Jews and British were being killed, his objective was to attack and claim the land surrounding the settlements – thereby affording protection. Techniques introduced by this courageous soldier continue to be in Israeli military use. Men trained by him included subsequent commanders, a minister of Defence and Chiefs of Military Staff. Because of the value of Wingate's unique contribution to the security and morale of the Jewish people of Israel, he is still held in highest regard fifty years later in Israel today.

We have seen the role played by Bible believing Christians in the restoration of Israel: Let us now turn to investigate the influence of the changed Christian attitude towards the Jewish people.

Notes

1.   Littell, F.H., *The Crucifixion of the Jews*, p.99.
2.   Cartwrights, *The Petition of the Jews for the Repealing of the Act of Parliament for their Banishment out of England*, London, 1649 – as quoted by B.Tuchman, *The Bible and the Sword*, p.121.
3.   ibid, p.144.
4.   ibid, p.178.
5.   *Psalm 137*:5–6 RSV.
6.   Tuchman, B., *The Bible and the Sword*, p.191.
7.   ibid, p.192.
8.   ibid, p.220.
9.   ibid, p.224.
10. Encyclopedia Judaica, vol.4, p.131.
11. Tuchman, B., p.312.
12. *Genesis 18*:18.
13. Sykes, C., *Orde Wingate*, p.112 as quoted by M. Pragai in *Faith and Fulfilment*.

Recommended reading

1.   *Bible and Sword*, B. Tuchman.
2.   *Why Pray for Israel?*, K. Burnett.

11

The Time to Favour Zion has Come

(*Psalm 102*:13)

'The purity and holiness of these men attracted me; their earnestness and the firmness of their convictions drove me to investigate their faith, which made them much better than myself or any people I ever knew.'[1]

This conviction of a Viennese Jew in 1843 is typical of many Jewish encounters with Christians recorded during the later 19th century. It marked **a distinctive change in the Jewish-Christian relationship and resulted in many Jewish people embracing Jesus of Nazareth as the Messiah of Israel.**

The Power of Righteousness

Contrasted with the harsh Christian experience of previous centuries of forced conversions and baptisms at the cost of banishment or death, a new Christian era emerged. We can trace this new attitude to the 17th century Puritan zeal to see Jewish people receive equal rights and be restored to their homeland. But more than this, these Christians were concerned for the Jewish people, which of course meant seeing them come into the fullness of faith in the Messiah. Jewish people came to desire baptism, but not forced baptism. Both the quality of personal faith and the availability of the New Testament played an essential part in presenting the truth of the gospel in its proper setting. This enabled the Jewish mind to understand the Jewishness of Christianity and to recognise a depth of meaning unknown to the gentile mind.

That the 19th century marks a turning point in Jewish people being 'grafted in' again is confirmed by the record of the Reverend J F de le Roi, (a missionary of the London Society for Promoting Christianity Among the Jews), in his book 'Jewish Baptisms in the 19th Century' published in 1899. According to his records, in that century 224,000 Jewish people were baptised. Upholding these facts but disputing the figures 'The Universal Jewish Encyclopaedia' (1941) states: 'These figures are manifestly too low . . . Actually the number of converts during this period must have been considerably higher.'[2] The encyclopedia lists some 200 eminent Jews of the 19th century, recognised for their notable contribution to human endeavour, who professed faith in Christ. Arthur Morse in his book 'While Six Million Died' records that in late 1938 'it was necessary to find new homes for 660,000 persons still living in Germany and Austria. Of this total, 300,000 were Jews; 285,000 were Christians of sufficient Jewish ancestry to fail the Nuremberg racial tests . . .'[3]

Statistical precision is not important for our purposes. The point established is that Jewish people were embracing faith in their Messiah to an extent not known since the early Church and that there were more Christians favourably disposed towards the Jewish people than there had been since the early Church period. The British 'Church Times' of August 17, 1883, published the following observation of the situation:

'There is reason to believe that there is no family of the human race which, on the whole and in proportion to its size, yielded more converts to Christianity.'[4]

One Jewish Christian, the Reverend **Elias Newman**, estimated that prior to World War II, of the 16,000,000 Jews in the world at least half a million professed faith in Christ. Newman further claimed that there were more than three times the number of Jewish Christian ministers than those finding their origins in any other non-Christian religion. There are also figures ranging from 250,000 to one and a quarter million Jewish Christians among the 6,000,000 Jewish people destroyed in the Holocaust.[5] Again, whatever the precise number, there is substantial evidence that there was a large body of Jewish Christians who ended their earthly pilgrimage in the crematoria of Nazi Germany. While Poland was the home of the largest Jewish population in Europe and sent the greatest number of Jews to the ovens, until 1939 Poland also was one of the centres of the greatest gospel outreach among the Jewish people.

Surpassing the importance of any statistics is the richness of the Jewish contribution to the Church. We should so expect it to be for they are 'the natural olive branches'. The shame is that gentile members of the Church have tended to overlook this fact, which is rarely found recorded in the history books. It is also significant that Jewish Christians (who understood both Judaism and the Jewish mind) were able to present Christ acceptably to Jewish people. Indeed, as they explain, many felt a compulsion so to do. We need to take careful notice of these men and their contribution.

Christ in a new light

Gentile members of the Church are indebted to **Alfred Edersheim**, a scholar and theologian, for his depth of research into the Jewish nature of our faith. Edersheim's writings give us **a portrait of Jesus as a Jew,** describe Jewish life in the gospel period and before, and illuminate the teaching of the rabbis. They also introduce the world of Jewish thinking and explain the sacrificial system and ministries associated with the Temple.

Edersheim explains his purpose in writing:

'I have wished to transport the reader into the land of Palestine at the time of our Lord and of His apostles, and to show him, so far as lay within the purpose of the scope of each book, as it were, the scene on which, and the persons among whom the event recorded in the New Testament history had taken place. For I believe, that in measure as we realise its surroundings – so to speak, see and hear for ourselves what passed at that time, enter into its ideas, become familiar with its habits, modes of thinking, its teaching and worship – shall we not only understand many of the expressions and allusions in the New Testament, but also give fresh evidence of the truth of its history alike from its faithfulness to the future of society, such as we know it to have been, and from the contrast of its teaching and aims of the comtemporaries of our Lord.'[6]

As a student in Budapest the young Edersheim was attracted by the New Testament when he discovered, 'the "Christianity" which I knew as such hitherto was not Christianity. What I did not know was the teaching of Jesus which opened to me such unfathomable depths.'[7]

The results of Edersheim's scholarship contained in his books – 'The Temple: its Ministry and Services as they were at the time of Christ', 'Sketches of Jewish Social Life in the Days of Christ', and 'The Life and Times of Jesus the Messiah' – continue as a rich legacy for all Christians interested in the restoration of gospel truth.

A fresh perspective of history

Where Edersheim illuminated the gospel for the world to receive deeper insight into Christ, **August Neander** presented the ongoing work of Christ in His Church in a dynamic thrust toward a predestined end. In an age conditioned by rationalism, Neander's clear presentation of Christ's working in the world in a continuum of predetermined purpose, inspired faith. To him the past was the beginning of a greater present and the preparation for a more glorious future – the past was the foundation of the building of the Church throughout the ages. His belief that Christ's constant presence in His Church was a power that would transform the world, penetrated all of his writings, engendering confidence.

In the preface of the first edition of 'A General History of the Christian Religion and Church' Neander stated his purpose in writing history:

> '**To exhibit the history of the Church of Christ as a living witness to the divine power of Christianity,** as a school of Christian experience, a voice sounding through the ages of instruction, of doctrine and of reproof, for all who are disposed to listen.'[8]

Following his baptism in 1806 Neander wrote to his pastor:

> 'My reception into the Holy Covenant of the higher life is to me the greatest thing for which I have to thank you, and I can only prove my gratitude by striving to let the outward sign of baptism into a new life become, indeed, the mark of the new life, proclaiming the reality of the new birth . . .'[9]

True to his word Neander defended the Christian faith against a tide of rationalist destruction threatening not only Germany but the whole of Christendom. Of him the 'Living Age' wrote in January, 1851:

> 'In the death of Neander, Germany has lost one of her greatest teachers, and the Christian world one of its greatest orna-

ments. A purer and nobler character has seldom adorned any church – one in which the loftiest powers of nature and the lowliest graces of the Gospel were finely blended, and which more fixed, therefore, at once the love and the admiration of all who came in contact with it.'[10]

Defenders of the Faith

Another defender of the Christian faith, extraordinarily descended from a family who escaped the terror and torture of the Spanish Inquisition was **Isaac da Costa**. A deepening awareness of the uniqueness of his people led to further study of Jewish history. He wrote:

> 'Throughout their history, both ancient and modern, I perceived something so extraordinary as to be quite inexplicable, unless we view the Jews as the subjects of remarkable privileges, and of as remarkable downfall; of a special election of God and of an enormous crime on the part of the elect people.'[11]

His strong convictions expressed in his courageous writings and speeches won him many friends among the nobility of his native Holland as well as in England, France, Germany and Switzerland and also attracted many enemies. Although barred from any university or government appointment, he was later appointed Poet Laureate in Holland. One Jew said to him: 'You would like to make all the Christians Jews, and all the Jews Christians.' This simply underlined the fact that da Costa **emphasised to the Church its duty and debt to Israel, while he proclaimed to the Jews Jesus as their Messiah**. Of him, the Jewish Encyclopedia comments:

> 'His character, no less than his genius, was respected by his contemporaries. To the end of his life, he felt only reverence and love for his former co-religionists, was deeply interested in their past history, and often took their part.'[12]

Carl Caspari's interest was arrested by Saul of Tarsus' persecution of the Jews. Intrigued by the book of the Acts of the Apostles he then went on to carefully study the New Testament. When convinced that this Jewish book revealed truth, he put his faith in Christ and set about telling his Jewish brethren and gentiles of his discovery. Later, recognised as an exceptional theologian, he wrote expositions of the Old Testament books and made a major contribution in editing a newly revised Bible in Norwegian. **Caspari's activity was considerably governed by his conviction of Israel's ultimate place in God's purposes.**

Although **Abraham Capadose**, a cousin to Caspari, was a physician, he also laboured in sharing his faith with Jewish people, particularly through his writing. He describes his encounter with the Messiah: 'One night I was reading in the prophet Isaiah; on arriving at the fifty-third chapter, I was so much struck with what I read, and clearly perceived in it, line for line, what I had read in the Gospel about the sufferings of Christ, that I really thought I had got another Bible instead of my own. I could not persuade myself that this fifty-third chapter, which may so well be called an abstract of the Gospel, was to be found in the Old Testament. After so reading it, how was it possible for an Israelite to doubt that Christ was the Promised Messiah?'[13]

David Baron was born into a Polish orthodox family, destined to become a rabbi. Burdened by original sin he struggled to find peace within his studies. Finally he found peace in Christ but rejection from his family – his father mourned for seven days for his 'dead' son upon hearing the news of David's decision. Baron's missionary zeal led him to the Jewish communities along the Russian border, in Germany, Austria, Hungary, Galicia and Bohemia.

Spreading their faith consumed the energy of many of these gifted men. Already we have referred to the work of **Michael Alexander**, the former rabbi who, as bishop of Jerusalem, established Christ Church. **Selig Cassel** served as a member of the Prussian Parliament which he relinquished to serve as preacher and teacher in a Berlin church. **Solomon Ginsburg**, the son of an honoured Polish rabbi, triumphed over intense opposition to establish many churches in Brazil. **Haymin Herschell** left his training for the rabbinate to teach the gospel to Jewish communities in London and Europe.

Leon Levison, born in Tiberias, was knighted for his political and economic contribution to Britain during World War I, distinguished for his work for the Russian Jewish Relief Fund. He was actively concerned for mission work among the Jews and the continuation of fellowship for Christian Jews which resulted in his forming the International Hebrew Christian Alliance.

Shabbetai Rohold was born in Jerusalem where he became a proficient Talmudic scholar, later moving to Scotland then Canada where he established a Christian Synagogue, finally returning to the mission station in Palestine. **Henry Stern** travelled widely with the gospel to Palestine, Baghdad, Persia, Abyssinia and England. **Joseph Wolff** also travelled taking the gospel to Egypt, Palestine, Syria, Baghdad, Persia, Greece, Turkey, India and England.

Further mysteries revealed

Many of the Jewish men who came to put their faith in Christ were sons of rabbis. Some had trained to be rabbis, while others had served as rabbis. Consequently these men had acquired an extensive knowledge of Hebrew, detailed learning in the Torah and the Talmud, as well as a deep knowledge of the prophets and writings. Such men knew the Old Testament at a depth not known by gentiles, and when they came to recognise Jesus as the Messiah they received revelation of God's purposes that equipped them for unique service.

One man's observations of **David Baron** serve to demonstrate the point. 'He found that the characteristic weakness of present-day Christianity is superficiality and shallowness. He searched to discover the main cause of this, and came to the conclusion that **"it is chiefly to the . . . fragmentary, vague, disjointed, textual manner in which the Bible is being dealt with that the lamentable lack of depth and backbone of Christianity today is due.** It is also owing chiefly to this cause, and to the neglect or misinterpretation of typology and prophecy, and the ignoring of the position of Israel in relation to the purpose of God, as revealed in the Scriptures, that the Old Testament has become 'as the words of a book that is sealed' to the majority of professing Christians." He therefore decided to unfold . . . whole Scriptures, and thus let the sacred oracles speak for themselves.'[14]

Raphael Biesenthal was born in Prussia of pious parents who intended him to be a Jewish scholar and rabbi – he achieved these to an exceptional standard although not quite as his parents had hoped. After being awarded a doctorate in theology and philology in Berlin he was baptised. He explains his call:

'My Biblical studies led me, after much searching and wandering . . . to find Him of whom "Moses in the Law, and the

Prophets did write." This result, this light which God caused to shine in my darkness, I deem it my unrelenting duty to communicate to others yet living in darkness, because the Lord Himself says that we should not put our light under a bushel. The apostles, as well as the Fathers, were furthered by the same disposition of mind. "For where your treasure is there will your heart be also," says the Lord. If Christ be our treasure, our heart must be entirely and undividedly His own, and all our talents devoted to the glory of His kingdom. . .

I have long considered it both a duty and a privilege to communicate to my brethren after the flesh the message of salvation, and to employ those talents which God has given me for their welfare . . . I should show my brethren from their very literature, as well as from the Bible, that the treasures of wisdom and knowledge are hid in Christ, and that we can only know the Father through Him . . .'[15]

Biesenthal's prolific writing made him a household name in Germany. He wrote commentaries on the Gospels, the Epistles to the Romans and Hebrews, and the Psalms; he compiled a Hebrew lexicon, translations into Hebrew of the book of Acts and Romans. In his 'History of the Christian Church' **he wrote especially for Jews showing the Jewishness of the early Church.**

Isidor Lowenthal was sent as a missionary to Afghanistan where he rapidly attained great understanding of the language. Not only did he translate the New Testament into Pushtu – the chief language of Afghanistan and parts of India, but he also compiled a dictionary in Pushtu which was left in manuscript form when he was shot by his servant after only seven years in the country at 38 years of age.

Isaac Salkinson from Lithuania expressed a deep concern for his own people. His first experience of the New Testament gave him a clear vision of his life's work: **'When for the first time in my life I read the New Testament, it was a Hebrew version. I felt then how great a necessity there was for a version in idiomatic Hebrew.'**[16]

In his endeavours to present the fullness of God's plan for man to the Jewish people he firstly published 'The Philosophy of the Plan of Salvation' which he translated into Hebrew. He then translated into Hebrew Milton's 'Paradise Lost'. Salkinson's greatest achievement and satisfaction was translating the Greek New Testament into idiomatic Hebrew. Before his death he wrote: 'My Hebrew version of the New Testament is now ready for publication. Hebrew translation seems to be the only talent given to me, and I have consecrated it unto the Lord. It is my alabaster box of precious ointment which I pour out in honour of my Saviour, that the fragrance of His name may fill the whole house of Israel.'[17]

Joseph Schereschewsky's outstanding ability in linguistics well equipped him for the remarkable saga of revising and completing the Bible in Mandarin Chinese and the Wenli dialect. After the Mandarin Bible was completed in 1875, Joseph was stricken by a serious illness which left him totally paralysed. Although he resigned his office of bishop, he continued his translation work on the Wenli Bible. His constant pain and severe handicap did not prevent him from persevering by training his index fingers to operate an English typewriter. On the completion of this remarkable task in 1895, he undertook the transferring of the romanised text of his Bible into Chinese characters. Undaunted, he accepted the American Bible Society's request to travel to Tokyo to supervise the printing of a revised version of the Old Testament in the Mandarin dialect.

Schereschewsky's translation of the Bible into these dialects made the scriptures available to a potential 250,000,000 people. In addition to preparing a concordance in Chinese for the entire Bible he wrote grammars and dictionaries to assist in the study of Chinese. It was said of him: 'Schereschewsky is one of the six most learned Orientalists in the world.'[18] The Reverend William Stevens expressed the following tribute:

> 'The grandest conquests of the world's mightiest heroes sink into littleness beside the work of Bishop Schereschewsky . . . when he made the Bible speak in Mandarin and heralded out salvation over half a hemisphere.'[19]

Bible translators are dependent upon accurate texts. Originally Jewish scribes laboured upon the writing of the scriptures by hand as the only means of transmission. Regardless of the care taken, mistakes were made as they earnestly endeavoured to preserve an accurate record of the Old Testament. The Jewish scholars who checked these scriptures made marginal notes where corrections were necessary. Between the 6th and 9th centuries A.D. these notes were for the first time collated and considered for correct spelling and word pronunciation – a vital detailed analysis essential for accurate Bible translation.

David Ginsburg, of Polish descent, completed an extensive study and published the amended Hebrew text. He was elected to the Board of Old Testament Revisers and he searched to recover all the notes available from these Jewish scholars – the Massorah. Ginsburg handled a large volume of the textual criticism which he finally published in one volume. This work has enabled Bible scholars and translators to consider how far the old manuscripts agree in their variations, additions and deficiencies.

The long list of Jewish Christians actively sharing the new light of their faith encompasses many varied places in society – Britain's empire-building prime minister, **Benjamin Disraeli**; Germany's illustrious musician and composer, **Felix Mendelssohn**; England's astronomer **William Herschel**. The list includes teachers, writers, church builders and leaders – **Isaac Helmuth** of Poland; **Ludwig Jacoby, Freidrich Philippi, Freidrich Stahl** and **Max Wertheimer** of Germany; **Christian Kalkar** of Sweden; **Julius Kobner** of Denmark; **Aaron Saphir, Iechiel Lichtenstein** and **Charles Schonberger** of Hungary; **Joseph Rabinowitz** of Russia.

Is it a coincidence that this Jewish revival of interest in Jesus of Nazareth blossomed at the time Jewish people began to leave eastern Europe to settle in their promised homeland? Is it by chance that Herzl and the Zionists emerged onto the stage of history at this time in the wake of this movement, clamouring for their homeland? Is it incidental that by mid-20th century the Jewish homeland was internationally recognised as a State? Is it an accident of history that the 19th century Christian outreach to the Jewish people was followed by revivals of increasing magnitude during the 20th century?

No! **These events are not by coincidence, chance, incidence or accident – they are the unfolding plan and purpose of God triggered off by obedience to His principles.** Paul revealed the truth when he said, '. . . salvation has come to the Gentiles to make Israel envious.'[20]

This was the precise fulfilment of God's covenant with His people:

'When all these blessings and curses I have set before you come upon you and you take them to heart wherever the Lord your God

144

disperses you among the nations, and when you and your children return to the Lord your God and obey him with all your heart and with all your soul according to everything I command you today, then the Lord your God will restore your fortunes and have compassion on you and gather you again from all the nations where he scattered you. Even if you have been banished to the most distant land under the heavens, from there the Lord your God will gather you and bring you back. He will bring you to the land that belonged to your fathers, and you will take possession of it. He will make you more prosperous and numerous than your fathers. The Lord your God will circumcise your hearts and the hearts of your descendants, so that you may love him with all your heart and with all your soul, and live. The Lord your God will put all these curses on your enemies who hate and persecute you.'[21]

Notes

1. Comment by the Reverend Wingate about Edersheim as quoted by Gartenhaus, J., *Famous Hebrew Christians*, p.76.
2. ibid, p.23.
3. Morse, A.D., *While Six Million Died*, p.218.
4. Gartenhaus, J., *Famous Hebrew Christians*, p.24.
5. ibid, footnote p.25.
6. Edersheim, A., *Sketches of Jewish Social Life*, p.V.
7. Gartenhaus, J., p.76.
8. ibid, p.139.
9. ibid, p.135–136.
10. ibid, p.141.
11. ibid, p.62.
12. ibid, p.66.
13. ibid, p.50.
14. ibid, p.43.
15. ibid, p.46.
16. ibid, p.163.
17. ibid, p.163.
18. ibid, p.174.
19. ibid, p.175.
20. *Romans 11*:11.
21. *Deuteronomy 30*:1–7.

Recommended reading

1. *Famous Hebrew Christians*, Jacob Gartenhaus.

12

Israel Regathered by God

(Jeremiah 31:10)

On June 7th, 1981, Israel despatched a flight of F15 and F16 fighter aircraft at 4.40 pm local time, with orders to knock out Iraq's $260 million nuclear-research reactor. Israel reasoned that her implacable enemy would soon be making nuclear bombs. At 5.10 pm the lead fighter penetrated Iraqi airspace and at 5.30 pm they attacked their target.

'Time' magazine provided a thorough covering of the event. The Publisher's Letter raised the question of Israel's constant appearance before the world:

'In its first cover story on Israel, dated August 16, 1948, TIME hailed the newborn nation and its Prime Minister, David Ben-Gurion, with some prophetic words: "Although, in years to come fighting might break out again and again . . . it was time to stop pondering the settled question of whether there would be a Jewish State, time to start asking what kind of a nation Israel was" . . . As a result, Israel and its role in the Middle East have been subjects of 35 TIME cover stories, more than any other country or geographic area except the Soviet Union.

. . . says Bureau Chief David Aikman: "There is something almost cosmic about Israel's conflict with its neighbours. Where else in the world would the chief of the Air Force quote the Bible in answer to a reporter's question?" '[1]

Mr Aikman points to the unique character of Israel and to the only source for hope and understanding of what is taking place in Israel and the Middle East – the BIBLE!

The Publisher's Letter underlines the fact that Israel is constantly in the news and frequently the centre of it. God said this would be so. In fact He declared it about 2,800 years ago:

'In that day the Lord will reach out his hand a **second time** to reclaim the remnant that is left of his people from Assyria, from

147

Lower Egypt, from Upper Egypt, from Cush, from Elam, from Babylonia, from Hamath and from the islands of the sea.

He will raise a banner for the nations and gather the exiles of Israel; he will assemble the scattered people of Judah from the four quarters of the earth.'[2]

God makes two unique statements of what He will do uniquely with His people Israel. He says He will regather them a second time from the places He has scattered them and He will raise a banner for the nations by the regathering of Israel.

We know that following their 70 year exile in Babylon there was a regathering of the Jewish remnant under Nehemiah in the sixth century B.C. In the scripture quoted from Isaiah 11 the Lord is referring to a second regathering.

Since the return from Babylon there has never been an occasion in history until this century when a large body of Jewish people have returned to Israel.

Wave the flag for all to see

What is a banner? It is a flag bearing symbols immediately identifying whom, or what, it represents. When the blue flag with Union Jack and Southern Cross was unfurled at the Olympics the kiwis cheered. Every New Zealander present shouted excitedly.

God said, 'I'm going to raise a flag and everybody is going to see it! Everybody is going to know Israel is here!' But, only those who know the meaning of the symbol will know who put the flag there and why it is there.

To ensure that we know what He is saying without any doubt in our minds, God specifies from where He will regather this remnant – 'the four quarters of the earth'. He wants us to be very sure that this regathering is not confused with His first regathering from Babylon which would have been from one corner of the earth.

It is important to note Who is bringing the Jewish people to Israel. Isaiah said, 'the Lord will reach out his hand a second time . . .' Then in Jeremiah we are informed:

'Hear the word of the Lord, O nations; proclaim it in distant coastlands: "He who scattered Israel will gather them and will watch over his flock like a shepherd."'[3]

The God of Israel, who scattered her, is now regathering His people to Israel and His purpose is to be a shepherd, caring intensely for His people. God, the Lord of history is drawing His people home. This is no human design or historic accident, but an unfolding of God's pre-ordained plan.

The TIME publisher draws attention to the constant focussing upon Israel which is apparent to us in our media daily, whether the subject be conflict with her neighbours, terrorism of her people at home or abroad, criticism through the U.N., comments on her economy, or dramatic rescues of her people from oppressed countries.

It is not only as though Israel were constantly in the news but rather that she invariably hits the headlines dramatically as the centre stage of events – with her rebirth on May 14th, 1948; by the startling victory and recapture of Old Jerusalem in the Six Day War, June, 1967; by surviving the Yom Kippur War, 1973; by the finesse of the Entebbe rescue, 1976; by the dramatic rescue of over half of the Ethiopian Jewish community, January 1985. God has raised her as a banner to the nations.

Clearly, the God of Israel is not content with just the regathering of the Jewish people to their homeland, but **He wants all mankind to know about it**.

Don't you believe it?

The rebirth of Israel has had a marked impact upon the other two monotheistic religions associated with Israel: Christianity and Islam.

Many Christians have believed that Israel was finished. 'God has replaced Israel with the Church.' So they said, 'Israel's done!' Islam goes even further. Islam teaches that God has finished with both Israel and the Church. 'God has given His new truth to us!' they shout.

God was fully prepared for this one. He declared what would happen about 2,500 years before the event:

'Who has ever heard of such a thing? Who has ever seen such things? Can a country be born in a day or a nation be brought forth in a moment?

Yet no sooner is Zion in labour than she gives birth to her children.'[4]

What an embarrassment to those who said Israel will be no more. Then for the pessimists who said it wouldn't last long,

149

Israel has reached her 40th year. And to make absolutely sure He had silenced the critics **He planted Israel in the Islamic heartland where she belongs!**

> *'This is what the Sovereign Lord says: This is Jerusalem, which I have set in the centre of the nations, with countries all around her.'*[5]

With the blessing of God

At 4.30 pm Iyyar 5, 5708 (Jewish date), or 14 May, 1948, the National Council met in the Tel Aviv Museum Hall. Ben-Gurion, who presided, announced: 'I shall read you the Foundation Scroll of the State of Israel, which has been approved in the first reading by the National Council.' As he continued with the appeal, 'Let us accept the Foundation Scroll of the Jewish State by rising,' the entire audience rose. Rabbi Fishman thereupon pronounced the traditional blessing:

> 'Blessed art Thou, O Lord, our God, King of the Universe, who has kept us alive and preserved us and enabled us to reach this season.'

Ben-Gurion announced: 'The State of Israel has arisen. This session is closed.'[6]

> *Let the Name of Israel be remembered no more. (Psalm 83:4).*

The next day 650,000 Jews were surrounded by 40 million Arabs with one and a half million of them armed. Eighty thousand Jews in Jerusalem were cut off from the rest of Israel. **The miracle is that Israel was born and she was not and could not be destroyed.** The Lord had said,

> '. . . *no weapon forged against you will prevail, and you will refute every tongue that accuses you.'*[7]

It was at this time that, with their intended destruction of the new Jewish state, Arabs leaders called their people (the Arabs) to leave their homes temporarily. After the (later unrealised) Arab victory, they were to have returned. The Arab leaders thereby created the 'refugee' problem for which Israel has been blamed ever since. (See Recommended Reading).

TIME reported on August 16, 1948,

> 'Out of the concentration camps, ghettos, courtrooms, theatres and factories of Europe the Chosen People had

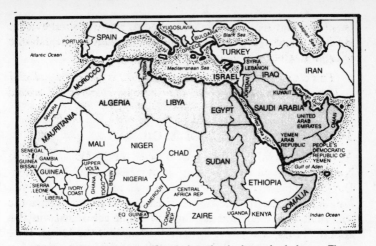

God planted Israel in the Islamic heartland where she belongs. The
dark areas are Islamic Arab nations.

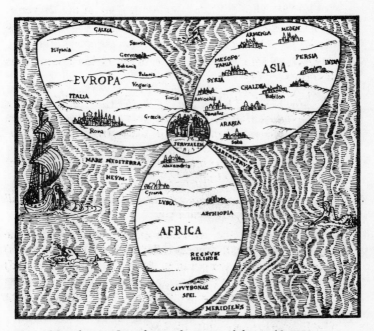

Map showing Jerusalem at the centre of the world: 1580.

*"This is what the Sovereign Lord says: This is Jerusalem, which I have set
in the centre of nations, with countries all around her." — Ezekiel 5:5.*

151

assembled and had won their first great military victory since 166–160 B.C. Israel's victory came after the worst of a thousand persecutions.'

Again prophetic words were fulfilled,

'Arise shine, for your light has come, and the glory of the Lord rises upon you. See, darkness covers the earth and thick darkness is over the peoples, but the Lord rises upon you and his glory appears over you.'[8]

Relevant Today

We have settled the question that God raised Israel for world attention. Why did God do this? We find the answer in the teaching of Jesus.

You will remember the events of Jesus' journey to Emmaus with Cleopas. Jesus explained His life and ministry from the Law, Prophets and Psalms,

'"This is what I told you while I was still with you: Everything must be fulfilled that is written about me in the law of Moses, the Prophets and the Psalms.'

Then He opened their minds so that they could understand the Scriptures. He told them, "This is what is written: The Christ will suffer and rise from the dead on the third day, and repentance and forgiveness of sins will be preached in his name to all nations, beginning at Jerusalem. You are witnesses of these things.""[9]

In doing this Jesus demonstrated **the importance and accuracy of the Old Testament** even after His death and resurrection. He is saying, 'All that has happened in my life to date, and that you have witnessed has been declared by my Father in the Law, the Prophets and the Psalms.'

The Covenants are related?

We have a major problem resulting in much misunderstanding created through the use of the terms Old Testament and New Testament. It is essential that we understand the importance of one of the most frequently used words in Hebrew scripture, **covenant**. In chapter 3 we studied the covenant God made with Abraham and the succeeding four covenants which developed from that covenant. We saw that the permanent New covenant replaced the temporary Mosaic covenant. Dr David Bivin sheds important light upon this subject.

'The best known commemoration of God's covenant with His people is called in Hebrew be-RIT mi-LA, the covenant of circumcision. In rabbinic literature this is also called "the covenant of Abraham our father".

Hebrews 12:24 speaks of Jesus as the mediator of 'a new covenant'. This is a reference to the well-known prophecy uttered by Jeremiah:

> *'"The time is coming" declares the Lord, "when I will make a new covenant with the house of Israel and with the house of Judah"'. (Jeremiah 31:31).*

However, **nowhere in the New Testament is the term "new covenant" used as a name for the collection of books which Christians refer to as the New Testament.** 'Scripture' for the early followers of Jesus meant the Hebrew Scriptures. The term 'New Testament' was coined much later in history.

Nevertheless, habe-RIT hahada-SHA (the new covenant), is the term used in Hebrew today to refer to the 'New Testament'. What Christians call the 'Old Testament' is referred to in Hebrew as ta-NAK. This is an abbreviation of the Hebrew words for the three sections of the Jewish Bible (to-RA, Torah; nevi-IM, Prophets; ketu-VIM, Writings).

Calling the Jewish Scriptures the 'Old Testament' denigrates the Hebrew Bible. 'Old Testament' seems to imply that the Jewish Scriptures have been replaced by the Christian New Testament, and that God somehow has abrogated the covenant he made with the Jewish people. Consequently, some Christians have concluded that the "Old Testament" is out of date and does not warrant such serious study as the New Testament.

Actually, the Hebrew adjective 'new' used with 'covenant' does not necessarily imply the replacement of an earlier covenant, but may only imply its renewal. Furthermore, the translation 'testament' in this context is unfortunate because it misses the connection with *Jeremiah 31*:31, and also may be misconstrued by the English reader to mean testament in the sense of last will and testament, rather than covenant.'[10]

Concerning the Law and the Prophets Jesus did not say they are null and void, but forcefully stressed their continuance until completely fulfilled:

'Do not think that I have come to abolish the Law or the Prophets; I have not come to abolish them but to fulfil them. I tell you the truth, until heaven and earth disappear, not the smallest letter, not the least stroke of a pen, will by any means disappear from the Law until everything is accomplished.'[11]

We have reference to the covenants by the writer to the Hebrews, he says,

'By calling this covenant "new", he has made the first one obsolete; and what is obsolete and ageing will soon disappear.'[12]

The emphasis here is introducing and seeing the fulfilment of the new covenant which is related to the old. The new covenant is not something totally different from the old, but rather it follows on from the former or Mosaic covenant.

Today we sometimes see old cars driven on the road. A car from the 1920s, no matter how carefully restored, simply cannot match a car of 1987 in performance, speed, comfort, and ease of driving. In 1920 they did not have the technological understanding of the 1980s, therefore, we expect improvement which makes the old version 'obsolete'. However, the old car has an engine that propels it forward on four wheels, directed by a steering wheel, gears that assist the engine load, an accelerator providing speed control, and a braking system. The 'new' version is a continuation of the principles of the old with substantial improvements through new revelation. In similar manner there is a continuing relationship between the former covenant and the 'new'.

Some people speak as though God finally gave up on the Law and the Prophets as though He had made a great blunder in His estimation of the people with whom He made the covenant. Then He decided to produce another covenant of a totally different nature with some other people. Thus God discarded the first covenant.

Firstly, such thinking does not agree with these words of Jesus who goes out of His way to forcefully explain that all God has declared in the Law, through the Prophets and in the Psalms, **will be totally fulfilled**.

Secondly, this thinking does not take into account the reliability of God's word:

'The grass withers and the flowers fall, but the word of our God stands forever.'[13]

154

or as God says on another occasion:

> '*Even to your old age and grey hairs I am he, I am he who will sustain you. I have made you and I will carry you; I will sustain you and I will rescue you . . . Remember the former things, those of long ago; I am God, and there is no other; I am God, and there is none like me. I make known the end from the beginning, from ancient times, what is still to come. I say: My purpose will stand, and I will do all that I please.*'[14]

Benjamin Disraeli expressed it this way:

> 'In all church discussions we are apt to forget the second Testament is avowedly only a supplement. Jesus came to complete "the Law and the Prophets". Christianity is completed biblical Judaism, **or** it is nothing. Christianity is incomprehensible without Judaism, as Judaism is incomplete without Christianity.'[15]

Getting things into place

Before His death Jesus told the disciples He had much more to explain to them, but that they had learned all they could understand at that time. He promised that the Holy Spirit would teach them in the future (*John 16*:12). After Jesus spoke with Cleopas He remained with the disciples for 40 days before ascending to heaven. During that time He taught them much that they could not have understood previously.

Following this time of teaching and empowered by the Holy Spirit, Peter explains to an eager crowd the significance for them of Jesus' death and resurrection and events that would precede His return:

> '*Repent, then, and turn to God, so that your sins may be wiped out, that times of refreshing may come from the Lord, and that he may send the Christ, who has been appointed for you – even Jesus.*
>
> *He must remain in heaven until the time comes for God to restore everything, as he promised long ago through his holy prophets.*'[16]

Jesus will remain in heaven until the time comes for God to restore everything to its rightful order. **The details of God's restoration programme are contained in the prophets.**

Since Jesus has not yet returned to earth the key to our understanding of what God is doing today lies with the prophets. When we turn to the prophets we find God telling us the accuracy of His word:

'I am the Lord, who has made all things . . . who carries out the words of his servants and fulfils the predictions of his messengers.'[17]

'. . . so is my word that goes out from my mouth: It will not return to me empty, but will accomplish what I desire and achieve the purpose for which I sent it.'[18]

'Then the Lord said to me, "You have seen well, for I am watching over My word to perform it.'[19]

'Surely the Sovereign Lord does nothing without revealing his plan to his servants the prophets.'[20]

Why did Jesus weep over Jerusalem?

Overlooking Jerusalem, part way up the Mount of Olives, stands a modern church, prominent for its unusual design. The roof is shaped like a tear-drop.

'As Jesus approached Jerusalem and saw the city, he wept over it and said, "If you, even you, had only known on this day what would bring you peace – but now it is hidden from your eyes. The days will come upon you when your enemies will build an embankment against you and encircle you and hem you in on every side. They will dash you to the ground, you and the children within your walls. They will not leave one stone on another, because you did not recognise the time of God's coming to you . . .

Then let those who are in Judea flee to the mountains, let those in the city get out, and let those in the country not enter the city. For this is the time of punishment in fulfilment of all that has been written. How dreadful it will be in those days for pregnant women and nursing mothers! There will be great distress in the land and wrath against this people. They will fall by the sword and will be taken as prisoners to all the nations. Jerusalem will be trampled on by the Gentiles until the times of the Gentiles are fulfilled.'[21]

Jesus wept over Jerusalem because He knew how the people's rejection of Him would affect them and the generations to come. As we have discovered, Jesus spoke of the fulfilment of the Law, the Prophets and the Psalms. He knew what they contained and He knew what their rejection of Him would mean for the nation of Israel.

Within a generation these words of Jesus completely described the dreadful events that occurred in Jerusalem. Under the orders of the Emperor Vespasian, Titus commanded an army of many legions that surrounded Jerusalem. Titus really desired the surrender of the Jewish people who were trapped within the walls of Jerusalem to come under the authority of the Roman Empire, but their intention was to offer resistance hoping for victory over the Roman army.

The Jewish people's determination to win was evident to the Romans in their heroism. Flavius Josephus, a Jew who turned himself over to the Romans, wrote accounts of the Jewish rebellion against Rome. His detailed reports show the accuracy of Jesus' words.

God's hand upon Titus may well be seen from an opening scene in the seige of Jerusalem where Titus finds himself ambushed by Jews. Lacking his armour Titus battled with his sword scattering his enemy while arrows rained over him although not touching him!

Jerusalem was cut off. The food supply rapidly dwindled. Jews turned against Jews in their efforts to survive. Jews lay dead around the city, unburied. All decency and restraint disappeared as hunger reigned. Wives robbed their husbands, children their fathers, and mothers from their babes! Food was snatched from the mouths of dear ones dying. Locked doors were broken open to steal food. People were battered to death for their morsels of food! Innocent victims were mercilessly tortured for their food, often by people desiring to store-up for themselves. Josephus says:

'To give a detailed account of their outrageous conduct is impossible, but we may sum it up by saying that **no other city has ever endured such horrors, and no generation in history has fathered such wickedness.** In the end they brought the whole Hebrew race into contempt in order to make their own impiety seem less outrageous in foreign eyes, and confessed the painful truth that they were slaves, the dregs of humanity, bastards, and outcasts of their nation.

. . .It is certain that when from the Upper City they watched the Temple burning they did not turn a hair, though many Romans were moved to tears.'[22]

157

Titus authorised the execution of Jewish prisoners by crucifixion in full sight of the Jews, hoping this would lead to surrender. The opposite happened. The Jewish leaders forced Jews desiring to give themselves over to the Romans to see their fate. The countryside was stripped of trees used for fortifications and crosses:

'The Romans, though it was a terrible struggle to collect the timber, raised their platforms in twenty-one days, having as described before stripped the whole area in a circle round the town to a distance of ten miles. The countryside like the City was a pitiful sight; for where once there had been a lovely vista of woods and parks there was nothing but desert and stumps of trees. No one – not even a foreigner – who had seen the old Judea and the glorious suburbs of the City, and now set eyes on her present desolation, could have helped sighing and groaning at so terrible a change; for every trace of beauty had been blotted out by the war, and nobody who had known it in the past and came upon it suddenly would have recognised the place: when he was already there he would still have been looking for the City.'[23]

It was reported that through one gate of the city alone 115,880 Jewish corpses were taken from the day the Romans encamped, April 14th, and July 1st. 600,000 pauper bodies were known to have been removed from the city and it was known there were many others not accounted for.

On August 10th, A.D. 70, the very day when – centuries before on 9th Av in 586 B.C. – the king of Babylon had burned the Temple, the temple was burned again:

'As the flames shot into the air the Jews sent up a cry that matched the calamity and dashed to the rescue, with no thought now of saving their lives or husbanding their strength; for that which hitherto they had guarded so devotedly was disappearing before their eyes.'[24]

Jerusalem was totally destroyed, not one stone of the Temple was left upon another. The Jewish people were defeated, crushed under the foot of the Roman army and those who survived were taken as slaves and scattered throughout the Empire.

As Jesus stood on the Mount of Olives overlooking Jerusalem, towards the end of His earthly ministry, he knew that it was now too late for a change of attitude – 'but now it is hidden from your eyes'. Jesus knew the dreadful suffering and destruction that would befall Jerusalem and its people in the future. That is why He wept. No doubt the words of the Law were ringing in His ears:

> *'If you fully obey the Lord your God and carefully follow all his commands I give you today, the Lord your God will set you high above all the nations on earth. All these blessings will come upon you and accompany you if you obey the Lord your God . . . However, if you do not obey the Lord your God and do not carefully follow all his commands and decrees I am giving you today, all these curses will come upon you and overtake you . . .'*[25]

Jesus wept because these 'brothers' of His had not responded to His teaching, they had missed their opportunity – 'but now it is hidden from your eyes . . . because you did not recognise the time of God's coming to you.' As we have seen this passage by Moses from Deuteronomy is an historical summary of what has actually befallen most Jewish people from the time of Jesus weeping on the Mount of Olives until today!

The Justice and Mercy of God

God is both just and merciful. God's justice would be meted out for disobedience to His will and purpose. God's mercy is also available to the penitent. Moses also declares God's mercy to the Jewish people when they return to Him (see the conclusion of chapter 11) and promises rich blessing:

> *'Then the Lord your God will make you most prosperous in all the work of your hands and in the fruit of your womb, the young of your livestock and the crops of your land.'*[26]

Some teach that God has finished with the Jewish people because of their disobedience. **It is clear from this portion of the Law that there is a way back to accomplishing God's purposes 'to set them high above all the nations on earth'. There is the promise of the restoration of their fortunes.**

Notes

1. TIME, June 22, 1981.
2. *Isaiah 11*:11–12.
3. *Jeremiah 31*:10.
4. *Isaiah 66*:8.
5. *Ezekiel 5*:5.
6. Keter Publishing, *History of the Land of Israel from 1880*, p.123.
7. *Isaiah 54*:17.
8. *Isaiah 60*:1–2.
9. *Luke 24*:44–49.
10. Bivin, D.,*Kesher: The Hebrew Connection* in *Dispatch from Jerusalem*, 3rd quarter 1987.
11. *Matthew 5*:17–18.
12. *Hebrews 8*:13.
13. *Isaiah 40*:8.
14. *Isaiah 46*:4, 9–10.
15. Gartenhaus J., *Famous Hebrew Christians*, p.73.
16. *Acts 3*:19–23.
17. *Isaiah 44*:24, 26.
18. *Isaiah 55*:11.
19. *Jeremiah 1*:12 NASB.
20. *Amos 3*:7.
21. *Luke 19*:41–44, 21:21–24.
22. Josephus F., *The Jewish War*, p.292.
23. ibid, p.303.
24. ibid, p.323.
25. *Deuteronomy 28*:1–2, 15.
26. *Deuteronomy 30*:9.

Recommended Reading

1. *From Time Immemorial* Joan Peters.

13

The Restoration of Israel

What did the prophets say? We have seen that Isaiah prophesied the return of the Jewish people from 'the four corners of the earth.' Isaiah gives us more detail about the promised return,

'Do not be afraid, for I am with you; I will bring your children from the east and gather you from the west. I will say to the north, "Give them up!" and to the south, "Do not hold them back." Bring my sons from afar and my daughters from the ends of the earth – everyone who is called by my name, whom I created for my glory, whom I formed and made.'[1]

God has made it extremely clear that He will regather the Jewish people from all over the world at a time in history which cannot be confused with His regathering them from Babylon in the sixth century B.C. Then they returned to Israel from a north-easterly direction but **this second regathering will be from everywhere.**

Michael Elkins, a BBC correspondent in Jerusalem, described the early years of the 'ingathering':

'They came from all of Europe, they came from Russia, from the United States, South Africa, Canada, Argentina, Australia, Iraq, Turkey, Iran, Tunisia, from the Atlas Mountains in Morocco. They came from places where most people hardly imagined that there could be Jews – from India, China, from the Hadramaut of Aden, from the mountains and jungles of Ethiopia. They came from 42 countries; from Western cultures, Eastern cultures, from tribal cultures as primitive as those of the Stone Age. They were monogamous, polygamous. They were doctors, lawyers, merchants, goldsmiths, witchdoctors, goat-herders. They hunted with blowpipes, with clubs, bows and arrows. They were Jews, all of them Jews.'

They come from the North

God commands the North:

'I will say to the north, "Give them up!"'[2]

A command, 'Give them up!" would only come if the people were being forcefully held back. A parent seeing his children bullied would shout with all the authority at his command, 'Give them up! Let them go!' In this way the Father of an oppressed Jewish people is commanding their oppressor, 'Give them up!'

When we look at a world map we see that **Germany is north of Israel.** Between 1935 and 1945 Hitler's systematic extermination programme killed 6,000,000 Jewish people, of which 1,000,000 were children! When the death camps were opened in 1945 the Jewish survivors set their course for Israel. The one thing in the heart of European Jews who survived World War II was to go to their homeland, Palestine, as it was known then.

It is of further significance that when one traces the longitudinal line north through Jerusalem it passes through **the Soviet Union** and particularly through its capital **Moscow**. Today it is estimated that there are approximately 3,000,000 Jews in the Soviet Union. Of these, 300,000 have applied for exit visas to emigrate, but have been refused. They are known as 'refuseniks'.

Jews who have applied to emigrate to Israel are severely penalised, either by losing their jobs, or by imprisonment on trumped-up charges. Some have been sent to grim labour camps in the Siberian wilderness for teaching Hebrew or for teaching the history and culture of Judaism. The release of Anatoly Shcharansky in February 1986 after 12 years of exile and imprisonment and much public protest from the west, and also that of Ida Nudal in October 1987 following a similar struggle for 16 years, are seen not only as a victory but also as bringing hope to many Jews in the Soviet Union. 'I will say to the north, "Give up!"'

Further emphasis and detail on this matter is given by Jeremiah:

'"So then, the days are coming," declares the Lord, "when people will no longer say, 'As surely as the Lord lives, who brought the Israelites up out of Egypt,' but they will say, 'As surely as the Lord lives, who brought the descendants of Israel up out of the

*land of the north and out of all the countries where he had
banished them. Then they will live in their own land."*[3]

The Jewish people every year for 5748 years have remembered their deliverance from Egypt under Moses by celebrating the Passover. This event marked not only their deliverance from bondage but also their establishment as a nation. It is almost too difficult to imagine the Jewish people annually commemorating another event which will eclipse the Passover. Yet the prophet declares that such a time will come when the Lord has brought the Jewish people home to 'their own land' from 'the north and out of all the countries where he has banished them.'

Reports from Christians scattered through the countries of Europe describe how both individuals and groups have prepared in various ways for migration of God's people through Europe. These people have acted upon what they believe to be the direction of God, quite independently of each other, in fact ignorant of other preparations. Food has been stockpiled, clothes gathered, accommodation prepared for large groups of people, ships and buses purchased for their transport, and Russian Bibles distributed – all awaiting a mass movement of people!

God had vividly foretold this:

'With weeping they shall come, and by supplication I will lead them; I will make them walk by streams of waters, on a straight path in which they shall not stumble; for I am a father to Israel and Ephraim is my firstborn.'[4]

An important aspect of their preparations in Finland, Norway, Sweden, Denmark, West Germany, the Netherlands, and Belgium, is that the programme has not been organised by a leader but rather, by individuals who have undertaken their projects only to hear later about others making similar preparations. Then they have realised they are a part of a large network. It is believed that this preparation is to receive an exodus of Jews from the Soviet Union – 'I will say to the north, "Give up!"'

However passages in Ezekiel 39 indicate that the bulk of the Russian Jews will not return to Israel until after the defeat of the Russian armies on the mountains of Israel.

'On the mountains of Israel you will fall, you and all your troops and the nations with you' (Ezekiel 39:4a).

163

'Then they will know that I am the Lord their God, for though I sent them into exile among the nations, I will gather them to their own land, not leaving any behind.' (Ezekiel 39:28).

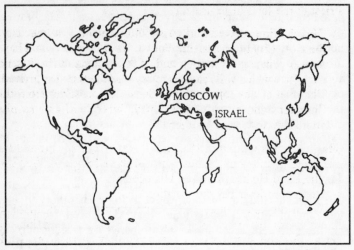

Map of the world showing Israel and 'The North' – Nazi Germany and the Soviet Union.

They come from the South

On January 4, 1985, world headlines reported that the Israeli government had undertaken **an evacuation from Ethiopia** of over half of the Jewish community numbering about 15,000 people, snatched them from a Marxist government, and settled them in Israel. This was called 'Operation Moses'. Over several years Ethiopian Jews, known sometimes as Falashas, had been flown out through Sudan, via Europe, to Israel. This exodus and release from Marxist oppression in a drought stricken country where they have been held in bondage, relates closely to the words of the prophet, 'I will say . . . to the south, "Do not hold them back!"'

I received a report from a contact in Israel who has worked among these new immigrants. This woman reported that time and time again these Ethiopian people explained that they have not left Ethiopia because of the drought – they have known drought and hardship throughout their lives – but that **they believe now is time for them to come home to Israel!**

164

One Ethiopian priest – they have priests, not rabbis, because rabbis are not mentioned in the Books of Moses (the Law of Moses) which they read, know and live by – wrote to the Chief Priest of the Jews in Jerusalem:

'Has the time arrived that we should return to you, our city, the Holy City of Jerusalem? For we are poor people and have neither prince nor prophet, and, if the time has arrived, send us a letter which will reach us to say that the time has arrived. The men of our country say, "Separate yourselves from the Christians and go to your country, Jerusalem, and reunite yourselves with your brothers."'

This letter was written in 1862 and it was answered, but not for 122 years! It shows us the heart-love of these people for God and for the Land He has promised His people.

The report describes the situation.

'When the communists took over Ethiopia, at first it looked like it was going to be a very passive situation for the Ethiopian Jews. For the first time in centuries they were given land, because under the communists everyone is equal. That was short-lived, for soon after that the communists outlawed Judaism and their condition became even worse than initially. As famine and drought increased, their neighbours blamed it upon them. We have many stories of men and women who were dragged out of their homes and were brutally beaten, torn apart and murdered, because they were blamed for the famine and drought – it was the Jews' fault, so they claimed!

Finally, they were being conscripted into the army and posted to extremely hazardous positions. So they wanted to leave Ethiopia to avoid the draft. Really and truly, the major reason for emigration is because they came to the realisation that they no longer had any chance to survive as a community. They knew if they continued in Ethiopia that their Judaism and their race would be finished.

To reach Sudan they had to trek through the mountains. In *Ezekiel 34*:25–31 God said that He would keep them from fear of wild animals because many times lions and beasts would attack them on their journey. Most of the time they had only a little water with them. Most any food or medications were stolen from them by robbers along the way. They had heard reports, from the young men, and young women, who had left several years earlier – the brave ones that made it through the mountains and wrote home – who said, 'Come, there is a road that leads through the mountains into Jerusalem.'

So, come they did. Again the younger ones would leave. Some of them didn't make it. Some of them were captured by soldiers. Some were sent back if they were not killed, beaten or imprisoned. Those who went back left again with larger groups: families, sometimes whole villages would pack up and leave.

When they reached Sudan they found out that they were not yet in Israel, in fact they were in a worse situation than ever. In Sudan they suffered more persecution and hatred from the Christians and the non-Jewish Ethiopians in the camps because food was so competitive, space was so competitive. Many of them tried to hide their identities as Jewish Ethiopians. Mostly they huddled together in their small huts, and every day was filled with fear. However, they did have one advantage over the other Ethiopians, they knew in their hearts they were going home. There was always the hope of Israel. So by an act of God, a real miracle, they were brought by aeroplanes to Israel.'

The hope of these people is promised by God,

'They will no longer be plundered by the nations, nor will wild animals devour them. They will live in safety, and no-one will make them afraid. I will provide for them a land renowned for its crops, and they will no longer be victims of famine in the land or bear the scorn of the nations. Then they will know that I, the Lord their God, am with them and that they, the house of Israel, are my people, declares the Sovereign Lord.'[5]

Origins of the Jewish Population of Israel 1975

Israeli born	Born in Europe & America	Born in Asia & Africa (mainly Arab countries)
1,506,300 51%	799,400 27%	653,700 22%

⬅ TOTAL 2 959 400 ➡

The Jews can't be stopped coming

Let us see how precisely the prophetic word has been fulfilled in God's regathering the Jewish people to Israel.

'They will return from the land of the enemy. So there is hope for your future.'[6]

In October, 1981, I heard Dr M Jaffe, then Chairman of the Union of Synagogues in Israel, describe his feelings when he visited the death camps of Europe in 1945. He said, 'If I were asked how long it would be before the Jewish people had their own homeland, I would have replied, "Over one hundred years!" A third of our people had been carefully exterminated: scientists, physicians, teachers and lawyers were hunted and killed. If you were to operate on a human body and remove one third of his organs he would die. But that is what happened to my people! Today we are a nation! We have a university in Jerusalem, in Tel Aviv, in Beer Sheva and in Haifa. It's a miracle!' A miracle it is, as the prophetic word of the Lord has been established in history.

A further verse describes **the regathering after the Holocaust:**

'"Return, faithless people," declares the Lord, "for I am your husband. I will choose one of you from every town and two from every clan and bring you to Zion.

In those days the house of Judah will join the house of Israel, and together they will come from a northern land to the land I gave your forefathers as an inheritance."'[7]

Dr Derek Prince, who lived in Jerusalem following World War II, noted that this 'northern land' was the area from which many of the Jewish refugees came from, to Israel. Many times he heard survivors describe how they were the only surviving member of their Berlin family but since arriving in Israel had discovered a relative from another city, say Hanover. Many times he has heard a similar story with reference to other cities: in fact 'one from a city and two from a family' now in Israel.

Another distinct reference to a specific group of Jewish people whom God decreed would return to Israel as a part of **the ingathering are from China:**

'See, they will come from afar – some from the north, some from the west, some from the region of Sinim.'[8]

Lance Lambert points out that 'Sinim' in modern Hebrew means 'the land of the Chinese'. Jews have been reported in China as far back as the 9th century when 1,000 men, women and children migrated from either Persia or India. In the 13th century Marco Polo's reports indicated a sizeable community.

The rise of Nazism led 18,000 to 20,000 Jewish victims to China between 1938 and 1941, raising the population to about 30,000. Many of these Jews emigrated to Israel at the time of her rebirth.

Gentiles will prepare the way

God gives further insight into His strategy for their return after the Holocaust:

> 'I will beckon to the Gentiles, I will lift up my banner to the peoples; they will bring your sons in their arms and carry your daughters on their shoulders. Kings will be your foster fathers, and their queens your nursing mothers.'[9]

During the horrors of the Holocaust many gentiles, at great personal risk to themselves and their families, hid Jewish people from the Nazis and their informers, ensuring the preservation of Jews, and subsequently enabling them to return to Israel.

Today in Jerusalem at Yad Vashem (the Memorial to the Holocaust) an avenue of Carob trees provides access to the memorial hall. This avenue is 'The Avenue of the Righteous Gentiles' – a tribute to individual people and families of gentiles who are known to have protected Jewish lives from this demonic attempt to wipe them all from the face of the earth. A special medal has been struck by the Israeli government in recognition of the Righteous Gentile. Each of these Carob trees bears a plaque at its base naming the **Righteous Gentile.** We find there are many names, mainly from European countries, among them Corrie Ten Boom whose story is related in 'The Hiding Place' and Raoul Wallenberg who mysteriously disappeared when the Russians entered Hungary after Raoul had saved at least 100,000 Hungarian Jews!

When the Nazis moved into **Denmark,** making the usual announcement that Jews were to wear a yellow star of David as a means of ready identification in preparation for their extermination, King Christian declared that all the citizens of Denmark are Danes and all shall wear the yellow star. The Danish Jews,

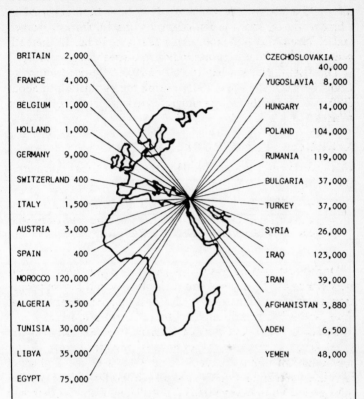

BRITAIN	2,000		CZECHOSLOVAKIA		40,000
FRANCE	4,000		YUGOSLAVIA	8,000	
BELGIUM	1,000		HUNGARY	14,000	
HOLLAND	1,000		POLAND	104,000	
GERMANY	9,000		RUMANIA	119,000	
SWITZERLAND	400		BULGARIA	37,000	
ITALY	1,500		TURKEY	37,000	
AUSTRIA	3,000		SYRIA	26,000	
SPAIN	400		IRAQ	123,000	
MOROCCO	120,000		IRAN	39,000	
ALGERIA	3,500		AFGHANISTAN	3,880	
TUNISIA	30,000		ADEN	6,500	
LIBYA	35,000		YEMEN	48,000	
EGYPT	75,000				

The Return of the Jews to Israel
1948—1964

"'In that day,' declares the Lord Almighty, 'I will break the yoke off their necks and will tear off their bonds; no longer will foreigners enslave them. Instead, they will serve the Lord their God and David their king, whom I will raise up for them.'" — Jeremiah 30:8-9.

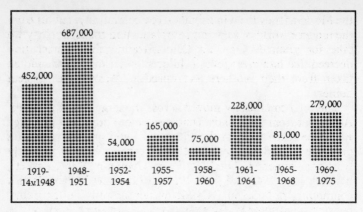

Jewish immigration – 'Aliya' – showing periods of immigration.

Population of Israel by Religion 1976	
Jewish	3,001,000
Moslems	402,500
Christians	89,500
Druse and others	56,000
TOTAL	3,549,000

thus concealed, were remarkably protected during the whole war. God said the gentiles would bring the Jewish people home and Kings would be their 'foster fathers', and that is exactly how it has been.

A Magic Carpet

A most unusual regathering from **Yemen and Iraq** is foretold in these words:

> *'In a desert land he found him, in a barren and howling waste. He shielded him and cared for him; he guarded him as the apple of his eye, like an eagle that stirs up its nest and hovers over its young, that spreads its wings to catch them and carries them on its pinions.'*[10]

In 1948 some 48,000 Yemeni Jews, from a community dating back to the times of King Solomon, began to move across the desert sands towards the British Colony of Aden. Persecuted by

170

the Moslems they lived in a feudal-type community, cut off from the modern world of cars and aeroplanes and the technology we take for granted. One law demonstrating their persecution decreed that fatherless Jewish children under thirteen should be taken from their mothers and raised as Moslems in Moslem homes.

The total community moved across the large desert to Aden. A prophet from their midst centuries before predicted that they would be taken back to the Promised Land on the wings of a great silver bird before the Messiah comes. That is precisely what has happened. The R.A.F., in 'Operation Magic Carpet', between June 1949 and June 1950, airlifted the Yemeni Jewish community to Israel in DC4 Skymaster aircraft. To the pilots' consternation some of the passengers lit fires on the aircraft to cook their food! The miracle is that they escaped from the hostile Yemeni regime.

From 1949 to the present day, about 130,000 Jews have fled to Israel from **Iraq** in three major movements. In the early 1940s they made the journey on foot; during the 1950s, there were a number of air-lifts and, in more recent times, during the 1970s, they have travelled by donkey through Kurdistan. Some had left considerable fortunes behind, and all arrived in Israel penniless after having their goods confiscated by the Iraqi government. Mordechai Ben Porat, a former Minister without Portfolio, left Iraq as a young man in 1945, he describes his adventure:

'I came overland by foot from Baghdad to Israel. I came with five of my friends from our underground Zionist movement, and it took us one month to get there. By 1949, I was a major in a combat unit in the army, and when I was released, went back to Iraq to smuggle Jews from Iraq to Persia, and from Persia to Israel. In order to get into Iraq in 1949, I entered as a Bedouin in traditional dress. In two-and-a-half years I smuggled 15,000 Jews. I was caught four times. Others were caught and sent to the gallows. I was tortured each time, finally escaped, and came back to Israel.

In 1979, after Khomeini returned to Teheran, I was sent to Iran to help the Persian Jews. We succeeded in getting about 2,000 Jews out. Just as the revolution was taking place, the 33 of us working there were rescued. I was in the Israeli Embassy seven minutes before Khomeini's mobs stormed it; for a week afterward, we fled from house to house until we were rescued by an American jet.'[11]

171

'Operation Babylon' took place between May 1950 and January 1952, when the American-owned Near East Transport company flew some 104,000 Jews – about 95% of Iraqi Jewry, and twice as many as had returned from Babylon in the sixth century B.C., from Iraq to Israel via Cyprus. The New York Times described it as 'the biggest air migration in history'. Former Knesset Speaker, Shlomo Hillel, under an alias, arranged this movement. Two years earlier he had managed to smuggle 13,000 Iraqi Jews from Iraq into Iran, and from there had flown them to Israel.

Israel offers these people a home and the hope of a new life as God has declared:

> 'This is what the Sovereign Lord says: I will take the Israelites out of the nations where they have gone. I will gather them from all around and bring them back into their own land. I will make them one nation in the land, on the mountains of Israel. There will be one king over all of them and they will never again be two nations or be divided into two kingdoms.'[12]

A Wilderness Cultivated

God not only declared how He would regather the people to 'their own land', but He foretold their activities on arrival:

> 'They will rebuild the ancient ruins and restore the places long devastated; they will renew the ruined cities that have been devastated for generations.'[13]

It is true that **they rebuilt the ancient ruins and repaired the ancient cities** on their return from Babylon in the sixth century B.C. after the exile which lasted seventy years. This does not refer to the rebuilding of cities which were 'devastated for generations'. The latter prophecy surely describes the second exile of the Jewish people since the destruction of Jerusalem in A.D. 70 and many even before then. It has been the devastation of about forty-seven generations that have been restored by those who have returned.

All over Israel the fulfilment of this prophecy is to be found, in the cities, towns and settlements. There are many examples – Bet Shemesh, Rehovot, Lod, Beer Sheva, Arad, Bet Shean, Tiberias, Ashkelon, Ashdod, Gath, Lachish, Ein Gedi, Gilo. These have all been rebuilt, either on the ruins of the former cities or beside them.

The next verse goes on to say:

'Aliens will shepherd your flocks; foreigners will work your fields and vineyards.'[14]

Young people from all over the world – **non-Jews – have gone to assist in the restoration of Israel**. Even today there are many young people who visit for several months; on a working programme, in kibbutzim where they are paid pocket money, and given accommodation and food, in return for working in the kibbutz industries. The industries vary but generally they are agricultural – orchards, flower growing, cotton, date and banana plantations – guesthouse work, quarrying and furniture manufacturing. Kibbutz Lavi exports synagogue furniture all over the world. Never before in Jewish history has this happened. Never before have gentile young people wanted to assist the Jewish people in such a way. It is noteworthy that most of the help has been of an agricultural nature.

Another unique prophetic word, that could never have occurred before in Israel's history was spoken by Zephaniah:

'Gaza will be abandoned and Ashkelon left in ruins. At midday Ashdod will be emptied and Ekron uprooted . . . it will belong to the remnant of the house of Judah; there they will find pasture. In the evening they will lie down in the houses of Ashkelon. The Lord their God will care for them; he will restore their fortunes.'[15]

Never before have Jewish people settled in Ashkelon. From its foundation until the dispersion of the Jewish people, Ashkelon has been a gentile city, formerly one of five Philistine cities. Ashkelon became a city in 1955. It was built from money sent from the Jewish community of South Africa and today is an attractive Jewish seaside city.

Costly Labour

It was essential for the survival of the first settlers that the land should be quickly made productive. High prices were paid for swamp and stoney land.

*'And the fields shall be **bought** in this land of which you say, "It is a desolation, without man or beast; it is given into the hand of the Chaldeans."'*[16]

Their task was arduous and the toll upon their life was high. Many returned to their former land. Numbers suffered malarial fever and died. But many persisted and through their sheer hard work saw a dramatic change from thorny wilderness and marshes to a thriving agricultural economy. The following description shows us what was encountered by these pioneers at the turn of the century:

'. . . At the turn of the century, Palestine was no longer the land of milk and honey described by the Bible, but a poor Ottoman province, a semi-desert covered by more thorns than flowers. The Mediterranean coast and all the southern half of the country were sand, and the rare marshy plains were fens of the malaria which decimated the sparse, semi-nomadic population, clinging to slopes and bare hills.'[17]

We add to this picture the vivid description of Mark Twain in 1869:

'Of all the lands there are for dismal scenery, I think Palestine must be the prince. It sits in sackcloth and ashes. Over it broods the spell of a curse that has withered its fields and fettered its energies. The hills are barren, they are dull of colour, they are unpicturesque in shape. The valleys are unsightly deserts, fringed with feeble vegetation. The Dead Sea and Sea of Galilee sleep in the midst of a vast stretch of hill and plain where the eyes rest upon no pleasant tint, no striking object, no soft picture. One may ride ten miles, and not see ten human beings. A blistered, naked, treeless land.'[18]

Although the work was hard and most of the Jewish emigrants were not manual labourers but professional men used to clerical and office work, including doctors, lawyers and teachers, the dramatic change in the land in a relatively short time is recorded by Winston Churchill in his comments following his visit to Palestine in 1921:

'Anyone who has seen the work of the Jewish colonies which have been established during the past 20 or 30 years in Palestine will be struck by the enormously productive results which have been achieved. I had the opportunity of visiting **the colony of Rishon-le-Zion about 12 miles from Jaffa, and there, from the most inhospitable soil, surrounded on every side by barrenness and the most miserable form of cultivation, I was driven into a fertile and thriving country**

174

estate. The scanty soil gave place to good crops and good cultivation, then to vineyards and finally to the most beautiful, luxurious orange groves, all created in 20 or 30 years by the Jewish community who live there.'[19]

God announced very clearly His earnest desire to take Jewish people home to their land which they would buy and receive the title deeds:

'*And I will rejoice over them to do them good, and I will faithfully plant them in this land with all My heart and with all My soul . . . "Men shall buy fields for money, sign and seal deeds, and call in witnesses in the land of Benjamin, in the environs of Jerusalem, in the cities of Judah, in the cities of the hill country, in the cities of the Negev; for I will restore their fortunes," declares the Lord.*'[20]

I have looked in wonder at the orchards of oranges, plantations of ripening bananas, acres of apples, avocado pears and dates, the long stretches of cotton fields, valleys of wheat and barley, and even at the desert producing lettuce, tomato, cucumber and capsicum all the year round. As well as a large scale agricultural industry there is also the raising of cattle as healthy as any bred in New Zealand. All this packed into a land the size of Canterbury or Northland.

The official Israeli handbook states the following under the heading 'Agriculture':

'Israel meets much of its food needs through domestic production, supplemented by food imports that are more than financed by agricultural exports. It is also in the forefront of technical development for agricultural production.

A national water plan was drawn up in 1949 to bring water from the north of the country to the arid wastes in the south, resulting in increased arable land. The revolutionary drip-irrigation systems developed in Israel in the 1960's have resulted in substantial savings of water by directing controlled quantities to plant roots. Agricultural production has increased, costs have been reduced and water losses kept to a minimum. Nearly half of Israel's 1.1 million acres of farmland are under irrigation.

Agricultural exports have grown from $130 million in 1970 to $520 million in 1983. Citrus exports doubled during this period, and exports of other agricultural products, such as flowers, avocados, tomatoes, strawberries, melons, and cotton grew almost ninefold, resulting from a policy of diversification.'[21]

God had decreed this remarkable restoration of the land and growth of productivity:

> 'But you, O mountains of Israel, will produce branches and fruit for my people Israel, for they will soon come home. I am concerned for you and will look on you with favour; you will be ploughed and sown, and I will multiply the number of people upon you, even the whole house of Israel. The towns will be inhabited and the ruins rebuilt. I will increase the number of men and animals upon you, and they will be fruitful and become numerous. I will settle people on you as in the past and will make you prosper more than before.'[22]

The Ingathering of the Exiles

The Declaration of Independence proclaims: 'The State of Israel will be open to Jewish immigration and the Ingathering of the Exiles'. Since the rebirth of Israel, the population has grown over six-fold, from 650,000 in May 1948 to over 4,100,000 today; almost half the increase came from Jewish people emigrating to Israel, that is, 'aliya'.[23] God said, 'I will increase the number of men . . . upon you.'

The Reverend David Pawson undertook a study of the rainfall in Israel during the last one hundred years. On graphing the figures he discovered that the periods when larger numbers of Jewish people made 'aliya' were the times when there was greater rainfall and that this was specially marked in 1948 the year Israel was reborn.[24]

Through the terraced slopes of the Judean hill country, cropping acres of grapes, the shepherds lead their flocks of sheep and herds of goats to good pasture:

> 'Again you will plant vineyards on the hills of Samaria; the farmers will plant them and enjoy their fruit . . . they will rejoice in the bounty of the Lord – the grain, the new wine and the oil, the young of the flocks and herds. They will be like a well-watered garden, and they will sorrow no more.'[25]

This restoration is not yet complete but moves towards total fulfilment. God is in the process of restoring hope:

'They will come and shout for joy on the heights of Zion.'[26]

This has already happened as oppressed Jews have arrived home, but this is just the beginning.

A Restored Language for a Reborn Nation

The traffic officer blew a sharp blast on his whistle. He raced up to me and cautioned me but I didn't understand a word he said; he was speaking in Hebrew.

One of my first impressions of Israel was of hearing the people speaking, shouting and singing in Hebrew. The street signs are in Hebrew. Advertising posters are in Hebrew. Conversation is in Hebrew. Newspapers are printed in Hebrew. Every settlement of any size has a Ben Yehuda street.

Eliezer Ben Yehuda was the man almost solely responsible for the restoration of this ancient language. Born in Lithuania in 1858, he was educated at the Sorbonne in Paris. Eliezer struggled with the question that if freedom could be enjoyed by the population of the Balkan nations, why could not the Jewish people enjoy that freedom.

Ben Yehuda wrote:

'In those days it was as if the heavens had suddenly opened and a clear incandescent light flashed before my eyes, and a mighty inner voice suddenly sounded in my ears – **the renaissance of Israel on its own ancestral soil.**'[27]

In 1880 he wrote to a young lady, who later became his wife:

'I have decided that in order to have our own land and political life, it is also necessary that we have a language to hold us together. That language is Hebrew, but not the Hebrew of the Rabbis and scholars. **We must have a Hebrew language in which we can conduct the business of life.** It will not be easy to revive a language dead for so long a time.'[28]

Eliezer's was not an easy task. He was warned against travelling to primitive Palestine leaving the comforts of Europe. His doctor opposed Eliezer's intention because he had contracted tuberculosis. Frail in body but extremely strong in spirit he settled for a mean life in Jerusalem where he began his lifetime's work.

177

Hebrew had not been spoken for about 2,000 years as an every day language. It had been preserved and used for worship in the synagogues and for studying the scriptures, similar to the Roman Catholic practice of using Latin for worship. The task involved a systematic construction of new words from modern vocabulary using linguistic patterns from the ancient language.

As an example to the Jewish State he decided that his children should not hear any language spoken other than Hebrew. Theirs was to be a model Hebrew home. That is exactly what the Ben Yehudas achieved.

Eliezer taught Hebrew as he wrote a dictionary recording the words he constructed and their meaning. He began to publish a newspaper which, in the early years, grew to about 200 circulation. In the newspaper he explained the new Hebrew words he had created as well as writing articles encouraging the formation of a Jewish homeland, giving ideas of how it should be formed and guidelines for the development of the settlements.

Opposition to his work was strong and readily forthcoming. The orthodox communities were outraged at his progressive views and stoned his office. So angry were they with him that they excommunicated him and refused to bury his wife when she died in 1891 leaving Eliezer to cope with five young children.

Undaunted, Ben Yehuda pressed on with his work. Due to the vision and efforts of this one man, suffering from a then incurable disease, and assailed on all sides, Jews now spoke, wrote and read a revived national language. There was a Hebrew press and flourishing Hebrew literature. In 1916 the census showed that 40% of the Jewish population spoke Hebrew as their first language.

In 1922 Eliezer Ben Yehuda died. Three days of national mourning were declared. As his body was taken to its last resting place on the Mount of Olives 30,000 people followed. With the proclamation of the state of Israel in 1948, Hebrew was declared the official language.

No other ancient language has ever been revived, let alone as the everyday language of its people, just as no other people have ever been dispersed around the nations, maintained their identity and been regathered as a nation in their homeland.

'At that time I will change the speech of my returning people to pure Hebrew so that all can worship together.'[29]

Exiled Natural Life Ingathered

When many trees are planted on barren land, not only do they provide shelter, but they also cause increased rainfall. Israel has planted nearly 200 million trees in the past 80 years. The climate has changed and these shady trees have attracted birds and insects.

Lance Lambert gives an excellent account of the natural life in Israel in his book 'The Uniqueness of Israel'. Today some 450 species of birds can be found in Israel, including eagles, ravens, storks, sparrows, rooks, gulls, bee-eaters and even pelicans.

Some of these are resident birds while others are migratory. Because Israel links three continents, large flocks of birds travel through in their season. The Hula Valley in north Galilee provides a glorious breeding ground. Flocks of hundreds of birds flying in formation in Israel's clear skies are an awe-inspiring sight.

Although Israel does not today have all the biblical animals, the traveller sees foxes, lynxes, ibex, gazelles, wild goats, jackals, wolves and there are reported sightings of leopards, hyenas and wild boar.

During the past ten years several wild animal farms have been established. Alligators are now ranched on the Golan and ostriches herded on the Golan and in the Negev. Animal husbandry has crossed the wild ibex with the domestic goat, creating the 'ya-ez', a hardy source of animal protein.

General Avraham Yoffe, the first Director of Israel's Nature Reserves Authority set about searching the world for animal species that once lived in Israel but have since been wiped out. Wild asses were located in the Copenhagen Zoo. Roe deer were found in a Dutch shooting reserve. Addax antelope were revealed in Chicago. All of these species were acquired and returned to the home of their ancestors.

The Mesopotamian fallow deer, which once inhabited Israel's northern woodlands, were air-lifted out of Iran in December 1978. White oryx antelopes were indirectly acquired from the personal stock of King Faisal of Saudi Arabia.

Many of these animals were brought home to Israel, and released into appropriate reserves – the desert animals to Eilat and the forest animals to Carmel, near Haifa. At these special reserves, the animals were released into protected sections of their natural habitats. They were encouraged to form natural herds, to interact socially, to eat natural foods, to adapt to natural parasites and to be wary of predators.

How long, O Lord, How long?

We could continue to record the remarkable events describing how the people were regathered and taken to Israel, and how they have developed the land of their inheritance. The question on the lips of some Israelis is, 'How long will we have this land as our possession? How long are we going to own it this time?'

Until a person has lived in Israel, one does not realise the significance of that question. It is true that many Israelis have the attitude, 'Nobody will take it from us again!' An admirable sentiment, often expressed with total conviction. Yet living in a land constantly alerted by the sonic booms of aircraft flying overhead, continually harassed by attacks from surrounding neighbours and an ever growing incidence of terrorism, the question is well founded, 'How long will we have our land?'

To better understand this question we need to know something of the Moslem hatred for the Jewish people and Israel. The hatred of the Jews instilled in the minds of the millions of people populating the surrounding Moslem countries is well summed up in this quotation from an official Egyptian school-book for nine-year olds:

'O mother of Israel! Dry your tears, your children's blood which is being spilled in the desert will produce naught but thorn and wormwood. Wipe off your blood, o mother of Israel, have mercy and spare the desert your filthy blood. Remove your slain, for their flesh has caused the ravens bellyache and their stink causes rheum. Cry, o mother of Israel, and wail. Let every house be the Wailing Wall of the Jews . . .'[30]

Referring to material like this, the Syrian Minister of Education in 1968 said, 'The hatred which we indoctrinate into the minds of our children from their birth is sacred.'

كيـف نستعمـــل نجمة اسرائيل ::

'*How to use the Star of David . . .*' (Iraqi daily 'Al Manar', June 8, 1967.)

This hatred is alluded to in the prayer of Psalm 83:

'*O God, do not keep silent; be not quiet, O God, be not still. See how your enemies are astir, how your foes rear their heads. With cunning they conspire against your people; they plot against those you cherish. "Come," they say, "let us destroy them as a nation, that the name of Israel be remembered no more."*'

Although this hatred which is expressed towards Israel and the Jewish people is so grievously painful, **the hope for Israel and her future lies securely in the God of Israel who declared:**

'"*I will plant Israel in their own land, never again to be uprooted from the land I have given them," says the Lord your God.*'[31]

Notes

1. *Isaiah 43:5–7.*
2. *Isaiah 43:6.*
3. *Jeremiah 23:7–8.*
4. *Jeremiah 31:9 NASB.*
5. *Ezekiel 34:28–30.*
6. *Jeremiah 31:16–17.*
7. *Jeremiah 3:14, 18.*

181

8. *Isaiah 49*:12.
9. *Isaiah 49*:22–23.
10. *Deuteronomy 32*:10–11.
11. BIPAC Publication, *Coming Home*, p.12.
12. *Ezekiel 37*:21–22.
13. *Isaiah 61*:4.
14. *Isaiah 61*:5.
15. *Zephaniah 2*:4–7.
16. *Jeremiah 32*:43 NASB.
17. *The Jerusalem Post*, January 8, 1969.
18. Twain M, *Innocents Abroad*, 1869.
19. Churchill W, Speech in the House of Commons, June 14, 1921.
20. *Jeremiah 32*:41, 44 NASB.
21. *Facts About Israel*, 1985, p.67.
22. *Ezekiel 36*:8–11.
23. 'Facts About Israel', p.104.
24. Pawson D, Speech in Brisbane October 9, 1985, *The Meaning of the Feast of Tabernacles*.
25. *Jeremiah 31*:5, 12.
26. *Jeremiah 31*:12.
27. St John R, *Tongue of the Prophets*.
28. ibid.
29. *Zephaniah 3*:9 Living Bible.
30. Prittie T., and Nelson W.H., *The Economic War Against the Jews*, pp.170–171.
31. *Amos 9*:15.

14

Jubilee

God means business – He says what He will do and He does it! In what is probably the most quoted passage concerning Israel's restoration – *Jeremiah 31* – God says that His covenant with Israel and her descendants could cease only if the laws which govern the sun, moon, stars and tides ceased to operate according to His design.

To reinforce His point God says He could reject Israel and her descendants if it were possible for us to measure the heavens or to search out the earth's foundations. The fact is clear that God will not abandon His created order and neither will we search out the foundations of the earth.

'The Apple of his Eye'

With such an enduring love for the Jewish people it is little wonder that God calls them 'the apple of His eye'.[1]

The pupil of the eye which is described as 'the apple of the eye' is the most sensitive external part of the body. Because it is so precious our Creator has given it special protection. Firstly, the eye is set in a socket. Rarely is the eyeball damaged by a hit in the face as this socket protects it. Then, above the eye grows a hedge to protect the vision from the effects of perspiration. Eyelashes protect from dust and fine particles. However, if fine particles enter the eyelid the eye weeps to wash away the foreign matter. As a final resort we blink.

What protection for such an important organ of our body! **The Jewish people are equally important to God and similarly have been remarkably protected.** As we have seen some of the organised attempts in history to destroy this people, we have to conclude they are 'the apple of His eye' – how else could they still exist?

The Sign of the Fig Tree

When the wiry branches begin to show their green shoots it's not long before the canopy of the tree is outstretched and life is restored to the once dormant tree. Birds and insects are attracted and a community has been reborn.

Jesus spoke of this:

> 'Look at the fig-tree and all the trees. When they sprout leaves, you can see for yourselves and know that summer is near. Even so, when you see these things happening, you know that the kingdom of God is near. I tell you the truth, this generation (race) will certainly not pass away until all these things have happened. Heaven and earth will pass away, but my words will never pass away.'[2]

On the occasion when Jesus spoke these words He was with the disciples who were admiring the temple stones. When Jesus spoke of the destruction of the temple they asked for signs indicating when this would be. In His reply Jesus lists many events and concludes with this reference to the fig tree and the trees. The fig tree coming into leaf is to be a sign of great importance!

Almost throughout scripture the fig tree has symbolised the nation of Israel. We are instructed to look at the nation of Israel in the setting of the nations of the world. **Last century, life began to be restored to the Land known today as Israel. At last the fig tree was sprouting leaves.**

Jesus said that the sign is to announce the imminence of 'summer' and 'the kingdom of God'. The seasons are often referred to in scripture and summer is known for its precious 'summer fruits'.

The Year of Jubilee

The full harvesting season, of course follows and there is an implication here of a fuller than ever manifestation of the power of God – 'You know that the kingdom of God is *near*.' The crowning seventh and final festival of Israel's 'feasts of the Lord' is Succot, the feast of Tabernacles – also 'The Feast of the Ingathering'. (Lev. 23:34–43; Ex. 23:16). Did not Paul underline, 'How much greater riches will their (Israel's) fulness bring!' (Romans 11:12).

To ensure that we do recognise these signs God has fulfilled them in an unmistakable remarkable way totally in agreement with His word. At the conclusion of the Basel conference in 1897 Theodore Herzl wrote in his diary:

'At Basel I founded the Jewish State. If I said this aloud, it would be greeted with worldwide derision. In five years, perhaps, and certainly in fifty, everyone will see it.'[3]

At this conference of a nation without a land came forth a national flag and a national anthem, Hatikvah – the Hope! Of even greater significance is the fact that **50 years from that date the United Nations voted on the right of the Jewish people to have a homeland. On November 29, 1947, a few months later Israel was proclaimed a State on May 14, 1948.**

The Law of God defines a 50 year period as a Jubilee:

'Consecrate the fiftieth year and proclaim liberty throughout the land to all its inhabitants. It shall be a jubilee for you; each one of you is to return to his family property and each to his own clan.'[4]

The command of God that people were to return to their land and that families were to be reunited was fulfilled in 1948. In spite of the British restriction on Jewish people returning to their homeland, a great flood of people including at least 700,000 forced out of the Arab lands, came home. Family

Theodore Herzl's diary entry at the conclusion of the Zionist Congress in Basel, Switzerland, September 3, 1897: *"In Basel I founded the Jewish State ... Maybe in five years, certainly in fifty, everyone will see it"*.

members were reunited in the land of Israel following painful years of separation. **The rebirth of the State of Israel was a fulfilment of the law of Jubilee**.

O Jerusalem

But that is not all. To be doubly sure that we recognise the sign of the fig tree putting forth its leaves, God fulfilled another Jubilee. This time it concerned Jerusalem. General Edmund Allenby led the allied army into the Ottoman Empire during 1917. With a remarkable dignity and humility he took Jerusalem without a shot being fired.

Menache Eliachar, a witness, described the event:

'Jerusalem was attacked most severely on Saturday, but by Saturday night all was quiet. We managed to see the Turkish soldiers, whose retreat, incidentally was remarkable. The Turkish soldiers did not riot at all – all they asked for as they retreated was "ekmek" – bread.'

Jerusalem's Mayor, Hussein Salim al-Husseini, was leaving the city, waving a white flag, when two sergeants met him. There are various stories of why they had strayed and what they were looking for. Eliachar says:

'They were informed that a surrender was taking place, in which the keys of the city were to be handed over to the conquering army. But the first thing they asked us was whether we had any matches. This scene remains engraved in my memory to this day. It was one of the most difficult moments – for ten days, they had cigarettes, but no matches, and they found no way of smoking. To see these two soldiers, ignoring the events around them, just to see them smoking – it's something I'm unable to forget.'[6]

Another description is given us by Lowell Thomas, a war correspondent:

'The outfit that was nearest Jerusalem at that time was the 50th London Division, made up of Cockneys very largely. And they had gone ahead of their lines of supplies and they were short of food. And one officer, an old friend of mine, Major Vivian Gilbert, has a cook and a sergeant who were awfully good at foraging and he got out a map and showed

186

them where he thought there was a village a couple of miles away, and he told them to try and find the village and see if they could get any food. Well, they sort of lost their way and . . .

He was a Moslem, he was the Moslem mayor, who came to surrender Jerusalem to Allenby's army. And the first representatives of Allenby's he met were the company cook and a sergeant. And he turned the keys of Jerusalem, he surrendered, actually, to the cook, and the cook said: "I don't want any keys to any Holy City. All I want is eggs for my officer." That's the story of the fall of Jerusalem.'[7]

General Allenby reached the Jaffa Gate, dismounted, desiring to enter the Holy City of Jerusalem as a pilgrim, not as a conqueror. He arrived on the first day of Hanukka and the Jews of Jerusalem were moved to powerful emotion.

Victoria Valero described the arrival of the 60th Division on December 9, 1917:

'We looked westward and saw a white horse and people applauding. The entire city had already turned out on the sidewalks. General Allenby entered, followed by eight riders on red horses, and behind them more horses and more officers, greeted by applause and cries of welcome: Everyone was shouting "Welcome".'[8]

Rivka Amdursky-Buxbaum added:

'They were so polite; they shared their rations, biscuits and everything. It was so joyous and happy. I saw Allenby on a beautiful horse . . . They told us he was a king. And everyone said: "Let's all go out and see the king". It seemed to me that perhaps he was the Messiah . . . They indeed told us that it was Redemption – not only the miracle of Hanukka but Redemption. We knew that it was so and hoped that we would be redeemed.'

Rivka continues her description as Allenby entered the Jaffa Gate of the Old City of Jerusalem:

'They opened the great gate for him, which was always closed especially during wartime: they'd closed it at night and opened it again in the morning. But on that day, it was wide open. When I saw him . . . I thought perhaps it was the

Messiah! So respectable, so upright, so handsome. People cheered and applauded. We knew the Redemption had come! How we yearned to be redeemed!'[9]

Aircraft of the R.A.F. 14 Squadron flew over the city dropping leaflets commanding the people to surrender. This was written in Arabic. Allenby's name resembled that of the Islamic deity and many understood allah had commanded submission. Some 2,500 years earlier Isaiah had said:

'*As birds flying, so will the Lord of hosts defend Jerusalem; defending he will deliver it; and passing over he will preserve it.*'[10]

The squadron's motto: 'I spread my wings to keep it.'

General Allenby accepted the handing over of Jerusalem from the Turkish authorities on 11 December, 1917, the day the Jewish people were commemorating the deliverance of Jerusalem from a previous occupation, that of Antiochus Epiphanes. It was the festival of Hanukka, or as named in John's gospel, the feast of Dedication (*10*:22), a feast of freedom. Many Jews believed Allenby to be the Messiah, so significant was the event.

On June 7, 1967, during the Six Day War, the ancient city of Jerusalem was restored to Jewish sovereignty. Jerusalem had been under Jordanian occupation from 1948 and no Jewish person was permitted in that area. This meant many were pushed out of their homes and no Jew was able to worship at the Western Wall, the retaining foundation wall of the temple site.

To the Jewish person Jerusalem is the most sacred place in the world. Ever since the destruction of Jerusalem in A.D. 70 Jewish people have lamented their separation from Jerusalem so vividly presented in Psalm 137 which has been sung often by Jewish people, especially during the last two thousand years:

'By the rivers of Babylon we sat down and wept when we remembered Zion . . . How can we sing the songs of the Lord while in a foreign land? If I forget you, O Jerusalem, may my right hand forget its skill. May my tongue cling to the roof of my mouth if I do not remember you, if I do not consider Jerusalem my highest joy.'

God commanded:

'*Pray for the peace of Jerusalem: "May those who love you be secure. May there be peace within your walls and security within your citadels."*'[11]

And so they did. They prayed for Jerusalem regularly for two thousand years! The Jewish people scattered around the world concluded the observance of their festivals with the words:

'Leshana Habaah Biyerushalaim'
'Next year in Jerusalem'.

At the joyful celebration of every Jewish marriage the Jewish bridgegroom breaks a glass under his foot as an expression of grief for the desolation of Jerusalem and the dispersion of his people.

The yearning to be in Jerusalem was expressed in historic betrothal contracts written in the home of Rabbi Levi Isaac of Berditchev. It was stipulated:

'The wedding will, God willing, take place in the Holy City of Jerusalem. But if, Heaven forbid, because of our sins, the Messiah will not have come by then, the wedding will take place in Berditchev.'

Jewish commitment to Jerusalem is portrayed in the words of Rabbi Jacob Emden in 1745:

'Every Jew has to promise himself to go and live in the Land of Israel and to yearn for the privilege of praying there before God's Sanctuary; and even though it is destroyed, the Divine Presence has not left it. So hear me brothers and friends, remember Jerusalem . . . and do not, Heaven forbid, think of settling outside the Land. It seems that to us that as soon as we enjoy some tranquility outside the Land of Israel, it is as though we have found another Land of Israel and another Jerusalem, and that is why all these evils have come upon us.'

In 1967, while fighting for her life, the Israeli government warned King Hussein of Jordan to keep out of the war. Hussein ignored the advice and it cost him Judea-Samaria, often known as the West Bank, which included the Old City of Jerusalem. The battle for Jerusalem was over! One newspaper reported the event as follows:

Premier, Chief Rabbis Pray at Western Wall
Mr Levi Eshkol yesterday took part in afternoon prayers at the Western Wall. He was the first leader of a Jewish Government to visit the site of the Temple since its loss 1,897 years ago.

189

The Prime Minister, robustly cheered by the tired but elated boys and men who had freed the Holy City, was accompanied by the two Chief Rabbis.

Earlier in the day, as soon as the road to the Wall was clear, the Chief Chaplain to the Forces, Aluf Shlomo Goren, came at an eager run, carrying a Sefer Tora. He recited a traditional (sheheheyanu) blessing, congratulating himself and all Israel, both within the Land and without, on having the privilege of establishing the age-old hope – and without their right hand having lost its cunning, or skill.

The Defence Minister, Rav-Aluf Moshe Dayan, came soon after and there he made his declaration: "We will not give up this place."'

The people had been returned to their land and families were reunited. **The reunification of Jerusalem fulfilled the law of Jubilee. The God of Israel again put His seal upon this historic event which no man was able to prevent nor to reverse.** God spoke through Zechariah concerning Jerusalem:

'This is what the Lord Almighty says, "I am very jealous for Zion; I am burning with jealousy for her . . . I will return to Zion and dwell in Jerusalem. Then Jerusalem will be called the City of Truth, and the mountain of the Lord Almighty will be called the Holy Mountain . . . Once again men and women of ripe old age will sit in the streets of Jerusalem, each with cane in hand because of his age. The city streets will be filled with boys and girls playing there . . . I will save my people from the countries of the east and the west. I will bring them back to live in Jerusalem; they will be my people, and I will be faithful and righteous to them as their God."'[13]

'The Fig Tree and all the Trees'

As the Holy Spirit has accelerated His work in the Jewish people, God's first covenant people, so He is dealing with the nations from whence the Jews have returned. Israel is a specific tree among the trees, or nations.

The fig tree is often linked in the Bible with the vine, both being numbered among the 'seven fruits' and symbolising prosperity and peace. The vine is also used as a symbol of the Church, and the fruit of the vine, grapes, are also among the 'seven fruits'. Throughout the nations are scattered the other

covenant people of God, the Church, and while the Holy Spirit
has been touching the hearts of Jewish people He has also been
restoring the Church.

Since the turn of this century, as her people are being restored
to their inheritance (the Land of Israel), so we have witnessed
revivals among the nations. The emergence of evangelistic ministries such as Billy Graham and Oral Roberts emphasising the
need to be born again, has coincided with the rebirth of the State
of Israel. Furthermore, there has been an unprecedented move
of God in almost all third-world countries. Along with the
restoration of Jerusalem to rightful ownership is a parallel deepening of faith within the Church. **The fig tree and the vine
cannot be separated but the Church cannot produce the fruit
that God is requiring from Israel.**

> '*Can a fig tree bear olives, or a grape-vine bear figs?*'[14]

**These are signs of a moving towards a day when the fullness
of God's purposes will be known, as both Israel and the
Church, the fig tree and the vine, receive their full inheritance.**

> '*The trees are bearing their fruit; the fig tree and the vine yield
> their riches. Be glad, O people of Zion, rejoice in the Lord your
> God, for he has given you a teacher for righteousness. He sends
> you abundant showers, both autumn and spring rains, as before.
> The threshing-floors will be filled with grain; the vats will over-
> flow with new wine and oil.*'[15]

Notes

1. *Deuteronomy 32*:10; *Lamentations 2*:18 A.V.; *Zechariah 2*:8.
2. *Luke 21*:29–33.
3. Lambert L., *Uniqueness of Israel*, p.131.
4. *Leviticus 25*:10.
5. Lossin Y., *Pillar of Fire*, p.55.
6. ibid.
7. ibid.
8. ibid, p.57.
9. ibid, p.61.
10. *Isaiah 31*:5 A.V.
11. *Psalm 122*:6–7.
12. *Jerusalem Post*, June 8, 1967.
13. *Zechariah 8*:2–4, 7–8.
14. *James 3*:12.
15. *Joel 2*:22–24.

Recommended Reading

1. *The Last Word on the Middle East*, Derek Prince.
2. *The Uniqueness of Israel*, Lance Lambert.

15

Pray for the Peace of Jerusalem

(Psalm 122:6)

'A real stirring is taking place in the Body of Christ – shaking the Body of Messiah in Israel from Eilat to Metulla . . . We see young people of indigenous Assemblies that God has raised up! Like "roots out of a dry ground". We are seeing only the first fruits of what is happening, an indigenous Jewish leadership.'

Fruit on The Fig Tree and God's Law In Hearts

That events have almost gone full circle is apparent from this statement made to me by a person who has watched the growth in Israel for many years. It has also been observed that there are more Jewish Christians today than there have been since the early Church period and the majority of these live outside Israel. Most of Jesus' ministry was in the north away from Jerusalem, the centre of conservative Judaism. In the north He discovered a greater receptivity to His teaching. For similar reasons today, the new covenant has been more widely received by Jewish people in the nations than in Israel. But there is now evidence of a definite turning of the tide.

As we remember the hard labour of Bishop Alexander in Jerusalem, we need to note two very important points. Although the Jewish observer, earlier quoted (p.86), commented 'the hill of Zion is not a likely place for a Jew to forsake the faith of his fathers' he fails to do justice to the bishop. It is true that the comment reflects the unlikelihood of Jewish people in Jerusalem easily accepting change, but Bishop Alexander had no intention of encouraging or forcing Jews to forsake the faith of their fathers. Following in the shadow of Peter, the apostle to the Jews, the bishop taught fulfilment of the real fathers' faith in Jesus of Nazareth – **there was no question of forsaking that faith**.

Continuing the ministry initiated by the bishop, his successors built Christ Church which was completed in 1849.

Providing a Jewish environment, styled on the synagogue, the church deliberately lacks crosses and statues, preferring to use Hebrew and Jewish symbols to identify the Jewish roots of Christianity. The front of the church resembles the holy cupboard in which the Torah scrolls are kept in the synagogue – inscribed on the doors are the ten commandments, the Lord's Prayer and the Apostles Creed in Hebrew. Under the stained glass windows, 'Adonai, Immanuel, Ruach Elohim' – Lord, God with us, God's Spirit, which gentile Christians have translated: Father, Son and Holy Spirit. Across the top of the communion table, 'Zot aso lezikroni', 'This do in remembrance of Me' – the words of Jesus as He established the New covenant.

Inside the Old City of Jerusalem, Christ Church attracts local Israelis and visitors to Israel, both Jew and non-Jew, because it is an important part of the history of Jerusalem. This building serves as a reminder to Jewish people of the faith of the builders and first ministers. They believed that the blood sacrifice required by the Law of Moses for the forgiveness of sin and the promised New covenant by Jeremiah, was fulfilled in Jesus of Nazareth. It also reminds Christian pilgrims of the significance of the Jewish roots of Christianity, the need for repentance over the Church's persecution of the Jewish people, and the common hope we have in the Messiah of Israel.

An associated work with similar direction was commenced during the 1920s in Jaffa. After the State of Israel was established, the minister of a mainly English-speaking expatriate congregation with a few Jewish Christians visualised a future indigenous congregation. Immanuel House is becoming the reality of that vision. In addition to 'the House', which is a hostel for visitors, there is a growing congregation composed of mainly Jewish Christians, with an almost entirely Jewish leadership. The vision recently broadened to include a study centre providing the opportunity for deeper understanding of Biblical faith, courses in leadership and counselling. Today this is functioning.

Such a spiritual awakening has not been witnessed in Israel since the last of the Jewish Christians were banished from their homeland in the second century. Throughout the land of Israel today there are congregations of Jewish Christians. Not only has the fig tree put forth its leaves but fruit is also appearing.[1] The day has arrived when God is writing His law in Israeli hearts.[2]

In the early Church the growing congregations held a common belief in the redeeming power of the death and resurrection of Jesus the Messiah, yet reflected some variations of interpretation and practice. So it is today, as the Jewish body of Messiah is discovering the meaning of its Jewishness. The practices range from congregations which observe the stricter keeping of the Sabbath, the festivals and wearing of kippa* and prayer shawl through to those preferring to recognise minimal Jewish observances. Yet, to each of them their Jewishness is important and they share the common concern, that all Jewish people enter into the New covenant and recognise the destiny of Israel.

The Stumbling Stone

Our study of the Church's treatment of the Jewish people has revealed grave injustices to the people whom God specially called for His own purpose and whom He preciously describes as 'the apple of His eye'[3]. The caricature of Jesus that the gentile Church has presented to the Jewish people has become a wall rather than a bridge between Christians and Jews. We certainly have not made them envious of Jesus[4].

But the problem has roots other than just those attributable to the faults of gentile Christians. Paul, the Jewish apostle to the gentiles, explains two important points:

(1) that when Jewish people centre their faith on Moses – the Orthodox Jew – 'a veil covers their hearts' but by contrast when their hearts turn to a hunger for the Lord 'the veil is taken away'[5]

(2) that 'Israel has experienced a hardening in part until the fullness of the Gentiles'[6] has come in –

God has hardened them and **only** God can soften the Jewish heart.

Peter, the Jewish apostle to the Jews, like Paul, adds further light on the matter. He explains that

Jesus is 'the living Stone . . . that causes men to stumble and a rock that makes them fall'[7]

At the heart of the issue is Jesus.

That there is a marked change today in the Jewish attitude to Jesus is reflected in contemporary literature. Many Jewish

---

* Kippa: the skull-cap worn by orthodox Jews. Some Jews wear the kippa only during meals and while praying, other Jews were it at all times.

people have told me that in their parents' generation the name of Jesus was not even spoken; but today in Israel the attitude has changed. Many books and articles about Jesus have been written by Jews. Pinchas Lapide, an Israeli scholar, undertook in 1973 a study of the image of Jesus in ten Israeli textbooks. He concludes that the portrait of Jesus is not marred by the experience of any subsequent Christian Jew-hatred. Jesus' Jewishness is taken for granted in all the texts but with differing conclusions as His purpose. Lapide writes:

> 'Although a few texts speak of the "divergencies" of Jesus from the normative Judaism of his time, references to his "loyalty to Torah", Bible-rootedness and his Jewish ethos predominate by far . . . With the single exception of the gospels – or their sources – which were correctly described as records of Jewish faith, the schoolbooks of Israel today without doubt contain the most sympathetic picture of Jesus that any generation of Jewish children was ever offered by its elders.'[8]

Another Jewish scholar, however, discerns the heart of the issue: 'Jesus can enter the sanctuary of the Jewish heart only divested of all his supernatural glory'[9]. In other words there are many Jewish people who accept Jesus as a very important Jew but cannot believe He is Immanuel – God with us.

An example of the anti-Jesus prejudice is apparent in the life of a Jewish professor who was brought up in an orthodox home. The dread of Jesus' name was instilled in him from early childhood.

'With an entire ignorance of what constituted Christianity, but possessing an ingrained aversion to it; an enemy of Jesus by accident of birth but without personal animosity'. The professor explains that in the presence of a gentile Christian he first learned 'to mention the detested name without self-consciousness, and presently with wonder.' He says that through this Christian friend he received 'the accolade of spiritual living based on the vital principle of an all-embracing love, a sentiment the doxologies I had chanted in my teens had never brought me. This man at one magic touch had crumbled my walls. I felt myself to be a Jew who was a Christian, a Christian who remained a Jew'[10].

It is not surprising then that, parallel with the early Church experience, the Jewish Christians suffer great pressure from the religious zealots who misunderstand their message. There are many Jews who believe Jewish Christians have forsaken their Jewish identity and therefore they seek to keep them from influencing the faith of other Jews – these are the modern Sauls of Tarsus.** Although we live in another century, the trials, the dangers and the triumphs are similar. Ahead of them lies the hope of triumph – when no one in Israel will have to ask of others whether they know the Lord, for all will know Him[11] – and the promise of resurrection life in all Israel[12].

Who is a Jew?

This is a perennial and critical question in Israel. One report shows us that, while the issue is between an ultra Orthodox minority and secular Israelis, it not only affects Jews in Israel but also in the Diaspora, in the nations. 'The Knesset this month had once more to deal with the complex series of issues governing religion and state broadly covered by the popularist title 'Who is a Jew?' . . . the issue was forced upon the reluctant party by its ultra-Orthodox allies . . . The danger of these moves and all they imply can spell a catastrophic division between Jews in Israel and in the Diaspora. They could also sound the death knell for secular Jewish immigration from the free world.'[13]

By law of the Land, anyone who can prove a Jewish mother is regarded Jewish and eligible for Israeli citizenship. By contrast the apostle Paul makes it clear that a true Jew is one who is descended from Abraham and has accepted the redeeming work of Jesus[14], and he even refers to himself simply as a Jew[15]. There is a rabbinic saying that 'one must not steal the mind of a fellow man, not even of a Gentile'[16]. Herein lies the heart of the problem confronting Jewish Christians. While the professor mentioned above, and the apostle Paul, were determined that their faith in Jesus did not stop them from being Jewish, but rather made them fully Jewish, so today Jewish Christians regard themselves as completed Jews or fulfilled Jews.

The Messianic body in Israel today is seeking to discover its Jewish identity, its unique contribution to the universal body of Christ. They battle an opposition of zealots who claim that they

---

** See Appendix 3.

have 'converted' to Christainity and are now therefore no longer Jewish.

It has been repeatedly claimed that 'missionaries' entice Jews to convert to Christianity by bribing them. This came to a climax when Rabbi Yehuda Meir Abramowitz subtly introduced into the Knesset, at a carefully chosen moment when a minority of Parliamentary Members were present to vote, a bill to make it an illegal act to give 'bonuses' or 'bribes' enticing Jews to change their religion. This bill became law on April 1, 1978. It provides five years imprisonment or a fine of fifty thousand pounds (Israeli) for the offence. The recipient of 'bonuses' is to be punished with three years imprisonment, or a fine of thirty thousand pounds.†

Often the extremely discrediting activity of the zealots has drawn a strong positive stand by local Jewish people in favour of Jewish Christians. Press reports indicate that this extremist opposition is generally not acceptable.

Yehudi Meshihiim are True Israelis

That there is a growing recognition in Israel of the Yehudi Meshihiim (Jewish Christians) is clearly demonstrated by the definition of 'Jewish Christians' in the standard Hebrew dictionary, ('Even Shushan'): 'a sect of Jews that have declared themselves Jewish in their nationality and in their allegiance to the State of Israel, and Christian in their religion'[17]. Although the definition does indicate a change of religion rather than a fulfilment of biblical Judaism, the statement is clearly that a Jewish Christian is Jewish.

During a recent court case, a Jewish Christian who was serving in the Israeli Defence Forces was questioned as to whether he was a member of the 'sect of Messianic Jews'. The various reports in Israeli newspapers of this case explained that the Messianic Jews are 'a stream of Judaism . . . that has strong links to the Land of Israel, its people and state, to Zionism and to service in the I.D.F.' The reports continue 'that he is a Jew by religion and a citizen of the State of Israel, with a Messianic belief; nevertheless, he opposes the conversion of Jews to Christianity and opposes missionary activity.'[18]

---

† See Appendix 4 for *Enticement to Change of Religion* law.

198

Another Jewish Christian responded to an Israeli newspaper who had named him as a 'missionary' in one of its articles. In his published letter he concisely described Jewish Christians:

'But who are the Messianic Jews? We are Jews and Israelis like all the other Jews and Israelis: We pay huge taxes, serve in the Defence forces in all kinds of units, come from a variety of (Jewish) communities and countries, live in cities, settlement towns and elsewhere in Israel. As befits Jews, we believe in God and regard Him as the most basic principle of this world, and therefore of our lives. Everything that is good and beautiful and lovely emanates from Him and is designed for His glory – and we also, as well as the entire people of Israel.

One other thing that characterises us is our belief in the Bible ('Tenach' – Old Testament) and the New Testament. This biblical faith, which began among the people of Israel, points to Yeshua of Nazareth, the Messiah of Israel. There are several thousand Jews in Israel today who share this belief. Why must we be slandered?'[19]

We have seen that in the 19th century Jewish Christians laboured to win their kinsmen to embrace the fullness of their faith in Messiah by emphasising the Jewishness of their faith, translating the scriptures (especially the New Testament into the original Hebrew), and using their Rabbinic knowledge to interpret the Christian Faith in terms familiar to the Jewish people. Although individual Jewish missions were established, they generally chose to work from within the denominational gentile churches. As most Jews in the dispersion regarded themselves as good patriots of the nations in which they lived, so Jewish Christians introduced a vital unique dynamic into the Church, while remaining loyal workers within the denominational churches.

By contrast, the Jewish Christians in Israel today are seeking to regain the position their counterparts enjoyed in the early Church. In the words of one Jewish Christian: '**The revival of modern Hebrew Christianity is marked by the attempt on the part of the Jesus-believing Jews to regain entrance into Jewish society.**'[20] We are witnessing another stage in the restoration of truth and rightful function of the Body of Christ.

One writer accurately points to the heart of the issue when he defines 'Christianity as the Old Testament explained by the New

Testament, while contemporary Judaism is the Old Testament explained by Rabbinic law'[21]. In seeking the restoration of full truth, the Messianic Jews of Israel are working for the restoration of **biblical** Judaism.

A New Visitation

Joel, the ancient Jewish prophet, spoke the word of the Lord to the Jewish people of an extraordinary revelationary experience that would be theirs in the fullness of time:

> '*I will pour out my Spirit on all people. Your sons and daughters will prophesy, your old men will dream dreams, your young men will see visions. Even on my servants, both men and women, I will pour out my Spirit in those days.*'[22]

This was fulfilled only in its first stage at Pentecost. A second stage is soon to follow – see *Zechariah 12*:10–11 and *Ezekiel 39*:29. Testimony is given today among Jewish people of the supernatural encounters experienced through dreams and visions which bear a common thread, although perhaps described in different phrases. People tell that they have seen 'the Messiah', 'the Holy One of Israel', 'a young man bearing thorns on His head', 'a suffering Man', 'a crucified Man', 'a Man so bright in appearance with bloodstained hands' – and that person is identified as Israel's Messiah, Jesus of Nazareth.

> '*You will arise and have compassion on Zion, for it is time to show favour to her; the appointed time has come . . . The Lord your God will circumcise your hearts and the hearts of your descendants, so that you may love him with all your heart and with all your soul, and live.*'[23]

Gentile Encouragement

Gentile Christians have participated in many ways in the restoration of Israel. Some of their activities have been more prominent than others. Many have come from the nations to assist as volunteers, not only to work in the kibbutzim but in hospitals for the elderly, for children, and for war veterans; as dentists; as doctors; as nannies; and even in the reserve army.

Companies run by believers have been established in Israel to provide employment and assist the Israeli economy. These include a building and contracting business, another which manufactures custom designed furniture, a printing and publishing company, a company manufacturing radio-components. These not only provide employment for local people, they contribute towards Israel's economy and, in one case, its high export earning has been recognised by Israeli government awards several years in succession.

Dr Douglas Young discerned a need for American Bible students to better understand the land of Israel – its archaeology, history, geography – and to understand the people of Israel. He saw the importance of students, pastors, teachers and scholars living and working among the people of Israel where they could better understand the Middle East situation. So he established the American Institute for Holy Land Studies which well serves this multi-facetted purpose.

In recent years gentile Christians from all over the world have visited Jerusalem during the feast of Succot, (or Tabernacles). This is the feast of the Lord that particularly includes gentile participation. Moses makes provision for the gentiles at the Feast, Solomon prays for the foreigners who come to worship the God of Israel at the Temple dedication (which was at the Feast of Tabernacles), and the nations are required to be present during the Feast of Tabernacles when Jesus is reigning from Jerusalem[24].

Many Christians have felt the call to be in Jerusalem at this time identifying with and showing their support for the Jewish people and the nation of Israel. These visits have also enabled Christians to better understand Israel's pressures and needs, to pray for the nation as they travel the land and to return to their homelands with a deeper appreciation of the truth. They have shared their experience with others and have encouraged Christians to pray more effectively for Israel. However, it is important to note that Gentile participation at other times and at other festivals was not absent, and its continuance is implied in passages such as *Deuteronomy 16*:10, 11.

A New Heart For The Church and For Christians

The Christian accusation against Israel concerning the veil over their eyes should rather be a prayer for the removal of that veil.[25] The problem is that often reference to 'Israel's blindness' is made with an air of superiority and even arrogance, in spite of

Paul's strong warnings and God's sovereignty[26]. The Church needs to be reminded of the grace of God at work among us:

> '*Just as you (gentiles) who were at one time disobedient to God have now received mercy as a result of their disobedience, so they too have now become disobedient in order that they too may now receive mercy **as a result of God's mercy to you**. For God has bound all men over to disobedience so that he may have mercy on them all.*'[27]

Now speaking of veils, let us look at the Church. The one fact that is apparent from our study of Church history is that most of the Church's vision is veiled from perceiving the truth of God's purpose and dealings with Israel. It would seem by Christian behaviour – noting Jesus' injunction, 'by their fruit you will recognise them'[28] – that the Church is as veiled from the fullness of truth as are the Jewish people.

When Paul taught on marital love he likened it to the love of Christ for His Church,

> '*Just as Christ loved the church and gave himself up for her to make her holy, cleansing her by the washing with water through the word, and to present her to himself as a radiant church, without stain or wrinkle or any other blemish, but holy and blameless.*'[29]

We stand with a deep stain upon us as the result of our behaviour towards the apple of God's eye[30], the people of Zion, and that stain has to be removed!

Jesus' command to any person bearing guilt against his brother was: 'Go and be reconciled to your brother; then come and offer your gift.'[31] During World War II Archbishop Roncalli was instrumental in saving many Jews from the Nazis. After the Archbishop, who was the Apostolic Delegate to Turkey and Greece, was informed of several thousand Jews to be sent to Auschwitz, he immediately made available thousands of 'baptismal certificates' for use for the doomed Jews without imposing any conditions. Thousands of Jews were saved in what came to be known as 'Operation Baptism'. [32] Later as Pope John XXIII he humbly acknowledged the guilt of the church towards the Jewish people and sought forgiveness in this prayer of repentance:

> 'We are conscious today that many, many centuries of blindness have cloaked our eyes so that we can no longer see the

beauty of Thy chosen people, nor recognise in their faces the features of our privileged brethren.

We realise that the mark of Cain stands upon our foreheads. Across the centuries our brother Abel has lain in the blood which we drew, or shed tears which we caused by forgetting Thy love.

Forgive us for the curse we falsely attached to their name as Jews. Forgive us for crucifying Thee a second time in their flesh. For, O Lord, we know not what we did.'[33]

What will your response be? God plans a glorious resurrection for Israel and He is calling Christians to be co-workers with Him in bringing about this earth-changing event. If we are to work in harmony with God there are several essential steps we need to take.

Praying For Israel

(1) **We need to repent of any anti-Jewish attitude or behaviour** in our own lives. We should pray for a repentant attitude from within our church fellowship. We must pray for a repentant attitude within our own town, city and nation regarding any anti-Jewish behaviour. Perhaps you have never committed any anti-Jewish act nor spoken anything anti-Jewish. You simply have been ignorant of anti-Jewish behaviour and have never realised God's love for the Jewish people. But, do you pray for the Jewish people? The prophet Samuel said to Israel:

'As for me, far be it from me that I should sin againt the Lord by failing to pray for you'.[34]

(2) **We need to pray for Israel and encourage others to pray.** You could collect together a group of people to pray in your home on a regular basis. Remember it does not have to be a large group. Jesus spoke of the power of two agreeing in prayer and of His presence when two or three meet in His name.[35]

'**Prayer for Israel**', a non-denominational teaching ministry for the Body of Christ, provides amongst other things up-to-date information for effective praying; teaching on **how** to pray; prayer conferences for collective praying and teaching; prayer and teaching tours of Israel and literature, video and audio tapes. Further information may be obtained from:

P.F.I., P.O. Box 1, Golant, Cornwall, England or from:
P.F.I., P.O. Box 1032, Palmerston North, New Zealand.

(3) **There is need to educate Christians regarding our responsibility to the Jewish people and Israel.** Your understanding can be improved by reading, and by listening to cassette tape teaching. The sharing with others of literature and tapes are good means of helping others to understand. Have you considered hiring a suitable video tape on the subject and inviting friends to view it in your home? What about arranging a guest speaker in your home or prayer group and inviting an audience for an evening? Suitable resource people and material are available from the above addresses.

(4) **Prayer For Israel are in no sense political** and encourage prayer also for the Arab peoples and the Arab believers, even though this is not our particular ministry.

Our repentant attitude and positive response is promised a fruitful harvest where the years of corruption will be speedily redeemed:

> '*I will repay you for the years the locusts have eaten – the great locust and the young locust, the other locusts and the locust swarm – my great army that I sent among you. You will have plenty to eat, until you are full, and you will praise the name of the Lord your God, who has worked wonders for you; never again will my people be shamed. Then you will know that I am in Israel, that I am the Lord your God, and that there is no other; never again will my people be shamed.*'[36]

Clearly, **there are two veils to be prayed through. The veil that prevents Christians from understanding God's immutable covenant with Israel and recognising our debt and responsibility to the Jewish people. Then there is the veil that prevents many Jewish people from recognising the Messiah and understanding the new covenant, and true Biblical Judaism. If we deal with the first veil, we can be God's instruments concerning the second veil.**

Jewish people have obeyed the following command of God, whether they have been in the land or out of the land, but Christians have, at their own peril, neglected the command:

'Pray for the peace of Jerusalem! "May they prosper that love you. Peace be within your walls and prosperity within your palaces!"[37]

Notes

1. *Matthew 24*:32.
2. *Jeremiah 31*:31–34.
3. *Deuteronomy 32*:10, *Zechariah 2*:8.
4. *Romans 11*:11.
5. *2 Corinthians 3*:16.
6. *Romans 11*:25.
7. *1 Peter 2*:4, 8; *Romans 9*:33; *1 Corinthians 1*:23.
8. Lapide, P., *Jesus in Israeli School Books'*, *Journal of Ecumenical Studies*, Summer 1973, pp.515–531.
9. Jocz, J., *The Jewish People and Jesus Christ*, p.262.
10. Jocz, J., *The Jewish People and Jesus Christ After Auschwitz*, p.165.
11. *Jeremiah 31*:34.
12. *Romans 11*:15, 26.
13. *Israel Scene*, Vol.8 No.8, August, 1987, Editorial, p.1.
14. *Romans 2*:29 and 9; *Galatians 2*:15–16.
15. *1 Corinthians 9*:20; *Galatians 2*:15.
16. Jocz, J., *The Jewish People and Jesus Christ After Auschwitz*, p.157.
17. Jocz, J., *The Jewish People and Jesus Christ After Aushcwitz'*, p.164.
18. United Christian Council in Israel Newsletter No. 152, 10 June, 1987.
19. ibid.
20. Jocz, J., *The Jewish People and Jesus Christ*, p.204.
21. ibid, p.215, quotig Professor Alexander McCaul.
22. *Joel 2*:28–29.
23. *Psalm 102*:13, *Deuteronomy 30*:6.
24. *Deuteronomy 16*:14; *2 Chronicles 6*:32; *Zechariah 14*:16.
25. *2 Corinthians 3*:14–15.
26. *Romans 11*:8, 17–25.
27. *Romans 11*:30–32.
28. *Matthew 7*:16.
29. *Ephesians 5*:25–27.
30. *Deuteronomy 32*:10, *Lamentations 2*:18 (A.V.), *Zechariah 2*:8.
31. *Matthew 5*:23–24.
32. Lapide, Pinchas E., *The Last Three Popes and the Jews*, pp.221–22.
33. *Catholic Herald*, May 14, 1965.
34. *1 Samuel 12*:23.
35. *Matthew 18*:19–20.
36. *Joel 2*:25–27.
37. *Psalm 122*:6–7 Amplified Bible.

Recommended reading

1. *Israel Today: View the Land*, Anne Dexter.
2. *The Messiahship of Jesus: are Jews Changing their Attitude Toward Jesus?*, edited by Arthur W. Kac.
3. *Why Pray For Israel?* Ken Burnett.

16

Israel's Spiritual Rebirth

God has promised in His covenants a glorious resurrection for Israel:

This is What the Sovereign Lord says

'This is what the Sovereign Lord says to these bones: I will make breath enter you, and you will come to life. O my people, I am going to open your graves and bring you up from them; I will bring you back to the land of Israel.'[1]

Life from the Dead

'For if their rejection is the reconciliation of the world, what will their acceptance be but life from the dead?'[2]

'Your dead will live; their bodies will rise. You who dwell in the dust, wake up and shout for joy. Your dew is like the dew of the morning; the earth will give birth to her dead.'[3]

An Immovable Rock

'On that day, when all the nations of the earth are gathered against her, I will make Jerusalem an immovable rock for all the nations. All who try to move it will injure themselves.'[4]

A Royal Diadem

'You will be a crown of splendour in the Lord's hand, a royal diadem in the hand of your God.'[5]

The Ruin Restored

'In that day I will restore David's fallen tent. I will repair its broken places, restore its ruins, and build it as it used to be, so that they may possess the remnant of Edom and all the nations that bear my name, declares the Lord, who will do these things.'[6]

'I will return to Zion and dwell in Jerusalem. Then Jerusalem will be called The City of Truth, and the mountain of the Lord Almighty will be called the Holy Mountain.'[7]

A Sign to the Nations

'I will give you a new heart and put a new spirit in you; I will remove from you your heart of stone and give you a heart of flesh.

On the day I cleanse you from all your sins, I will resettle your towns, and the ruins will be rebuilt. The desolate land will be cultivated instead of lying desolate in the sight of all who pass through it.

Then the nations around you that remain will know that I the Lord have rebuilt what was destroyed and have replanted what was desolate. I the Lord have spoken, and I will do it.'[8]

The Lord is my Light

'Do not gloat over me, my enemy! Though I have fallen, I will rise. Though I sit in darkness, the Lord will be my light. Because I have sinned against Him, I will bear the Lord's wrath, until He pleads my case and establishes my right. He will bring me out into the light; I will see his justice.'[9]

'Then your light will break forth like the dawn, and your healing will quickly appear; then your righteousness will go before you, and the glory of the Lord will be your rear guard.'[10]

In That Day

'He will swallow up death forever. The Sovereign Lord will wipe away the tears from all faces; he will remove the disgrace of his people from all the earth. The Lord has spoken.

In that day they will say,

"Surely this is our God; we trusted in him, and he saved us. This is the Lord, we trusted in him; let us rejoice and be glad in his salvation."'[11]

Destined for Resurrection

'Then Simeon blessed them and said to Mary, his mother:

"This child is destined to cause the falling and rising of many in Israel, and to be a sign that will be spoken against . . ."'[12]

'He will see of the travail of His soul and be satisfied.'[13]

"As the new heavens and the new earth that I make will endure before me,' declares the Lord, 'so will your name and descendants endure."' [14]

Arise, Shine

'Arise shine, for your light has come, and the glory of the Lord rises upon you. See, darkness covers the earth and thick darkness is over the peoples, but the Lord rises upon you and his glory appears over you.'[15]

Nations will come to you

'Nations will come to your light, and kings to the brightness of your dawn.

Lift up your eyes and look about you: All assemble and come to you; your sons come from afar, and your daughters are carried on the arm. Then you will look and be radiant, your heart will throb and swell with joy; the wealth on the seas will be brought to you; to you the riches of the nations will come.

Your gates will always stand open, they will never be shut, day or night, so that men may bring you the wealth of the nations – their kings led in triumphal procession.'[16]

Notes

1. Ezekiel 37:5, 12.
2. Romans 11:15.
3. Isaiah 26:19.
4. Zechariah 12:3.
5. Isaiah 62:3.
6. Amos 9:11–12.
7. Zechariah 8:3, 7–8.
8. Ezekiel 36:26, 33, 34, 36.
9. Micah 7:8–9.
10. Isaiah 58:8.
11. Isaiah 25:8–9.
12. Luke 2:34.
13. Isaiah 53:11.
14. Isaiah 66:22.
15. Isaiah 60:1–2.
16. Isaiah 60:3–5, 11.

APPENDIX 1

Roman Catholic Policy Change

(See page 14)

The Second Vatican Council (1962–65), called on the initiative of Pope John XXIII, also dealt with the attitude of the Catholic Church towards Judaism. A declaration, 'Nostra aetate' ('In Our Time'), on the attitude of the Church toward non-Christian religions, was formulated by Cardinal Bea and the Secretariat for Christian Unity, and was promulgated on October 28, 1965. It reads:

> As this sacred synod searches into the mystery of the Church, it remembers the bond that spiritually ties the people of the New Covenant to Abraham's stock.
>
> Thus the Church of Christ acknowledges that, according to God's saving design, the beginnings of her faith and her election are found already among the Patriarchs, Moses and the prophets. She professes that all who believe in Christ – Abraham's sons according to faith – are included in the same Patriarch's call, and likewise that the salvation of the Church is mysteriously foreshadowed by the chosen people's exodus from the land of bondage. The Church, therefore, cannot forget that she received the revelation of the Old Testament through the people with whom God in His inexpressible mercy concluded the Ancient Covenant. Nor can she forget that she draws sustenance from the root of that well-culti-vated olive tree onto which have been grafted the wild shoots, the Gentiles. Indeed, the Church believes that by His cross Christ Our Peace reconciled Jews and Gentiles, making both one in Himself.
>
> The Church keeps ever in mind the words of the Apostle about his kinsmen: 'theirs is the sonship and the glory and the covenants and the law and the worship and the promises: theirs are the fathers and from them is the Christ according to the flesh' (*Romans* 9:4–5), the Son of the Virgin Mary. She also recalls that the Apostles, the Church's mainstay and

211

pillars, as well as most of the early disciples who proclaimed Christ's Gospel to the world, sprang from the Jewish people.

As Holy Scripture testifies, Jerusalem did not recognise the time of her visitation, nor did the Jews, in large number, accept the Gospel; indeed not a few opposed its spreading. Nevertheless, God holds the Jews most dear for the sake of their Fathers; He does not repent of the gifts He makes or of the calls He issues – such is the witness of the Apostle. In company with the Prophets and the same Apostle, the Church awaits that day, known to God alone, on which all peoples will address the Lord in a single voice and 'serve him shoulder to shoulder' (*Zephaniah* 3:9).

Since the spiritual patrimony common to Christians and Jews is thus so great, this sacred synod wants to foster and recommend that mutual understanding and respect which is the fruit, above all, of biblical and theological studies as well as of fraternal dialogues.

True, the Jewish authorities and those who followed their lead pressed for the death of Christ; still, what happened in His passion cannot be charged against all Jews, without distinction, then alive, nor against the Jews of today. Although the Church is the new people of God, the Jews should not be presented as rejected or accursed as if this followed from the Holy Scriptures. All should see to it, then, that in catechetical work or in the preaching of the word of God they do not teach anything that does not conform to the truth of the Gospel and the spirit of Christ.

Furthermore, in her rejection of every persecution against any man, the Church, mindful of the patrimony she shares with the Jews and moved not by political reasons but by the Gospel's spiritual love, decries hatred, persecutions, displays of anti-semitism, directed against Jews at any time and by anyone.

Besides, as the Church has always held and holds now, Christ underwent His passion and death freely, because of the sins of men and out of infinite love, in order that all may reach salvation. It is, therefore, the burden of the Church's preaching to proclaim the cross of Christ as the sign of God's all-embracing love and as the fountain from which every grace flows.

APPENDIX 2

Profession of Faith – Renouncing Jewishness

(See page 73)

This Profession of faith, from the Church of Constantinople, reflects Christian hatred towards Jews and shows us the impossible situation for Jewish Christians who held precious their Jewishness,

'As a preliminary to his acceptance as a catechumen (one undergoing training and instruction before baptism), a Jew, "must confess and denounce verbally the whole Hebrew people, and forthwith declare that with a whole heart and sincere faith he desires to be received among the Christians. Then he must renounce openly in the church all Jewish superstition, the priest saying, and he, or his sponsor if he is a child, replying in these words:

"I renounce all customs, rites, legalisms, unleavened breads and sacrifices of the lambs of the Hebrews, and all the other feasts of the Hebrews, sacrifices, prayers, aspersions, purifications, sanctifications and propitiations, and fasts, and new moons, and Sabbaths, and superstitions, and hymns and chants and observances and synagogues, and the food and drink of the Hebrews; in one word I renounce absolutely everything Jewish, every law, rite and custom, and above all I renounce Antichrist, whom all the Jews await in the figure and form of Christ; and I join myself to the true Christ and God. And I believe in the Father, the Son and the Holy Spirit, the Holy, Consubstantial and Indivisible Trinity, and the dispensation in the flesh and the descent to men of the Word of God, of the one person of the Holy Trinity, and I confess that he was truly made man, and I believe and proclaim that after the flesh in very truth the Blessed Virgin Mary bore him the son of God; and I believe in, receive, venerate and embrace the adorable Cross of Christ, and the

213

holy images; and thus, with my whole heart, and soul, and with a true faith I come to the Christian Faith. But if it be with deceit and with hypocrisy, and not with a sincere and perfect faith and a genuine love of Christ, but with a pretence to be a Christian that I come, and if afterwards I shall wish to deny and return to Jewish superstition, or shall be found eating with Jews or feasting with them, or secretly conversing and condemning the Christian religion instead of openly confuting them and condemning their vain faith, then let the trembling of Cain and the leprosy of Gehazi cleave to me, as well as the legal punishments to which I acknowledge myself liable. And may I be anathema in the world to come, and may my soul be set down with satan and the devils.'

As quoted in 'The Conflict of the Church and the Synagogue' pp.397–398. James Parkes.

APPENDIX 3

(See page 191)

The accompanying notice, which was found by the author posted around the streets of Jerusalem in 1984, reflects both the anguish suffered by Jews at the hands of Christians over the centuries and a distorted understanding of the gospels.

NOTICE
ALL ISRAEL BEWARE!

The Crusades are not over – Christian missionaries are on an evangelical crusade for Christ. They are distributing and teaching their New Testament all over our holy land.

The New Testament

– teaches **ANTI-SEMITISM** – it says that religious Jews and Torah scribes are hypocrites (*Matthew 23*:13–29) and that pious Jews are serpents and vipers who cannot escape the damnation of hell (*Matthew 23*:31).

– is **BIGOTED** – it teaches, 'I (Jesus) am *the* way, *the truth*, *the* life, No man can come to G–d except by me.' (*John 14*:26).

–teaches **HATRED** for it tells its followers that a man must hate his father and mother and wife and children and brothers and sisters in order to be followers of Christ (*Luke 14*:26).

– is a gospel of **WAR** – for it teaches 'I (Jesus) am come to set a man at variance against his father and the daughter against her mother and the daughter-in-law against her mother-in-law. And a man's enemies shall be they of his own household' (*Matthew 10*:35–36).

– calls for the **DESTRUCTION OF THE JEWS** – it teaches that those who do not obey the gospel of Jesus will be destroyed (*2 Thessalonians 1*:8–9)

–claims that **TORAH** is for **UNGODLY PEOPLE, UNHOLY PEOPLE, PROFANE AND MURDERERS, PROSTITUTES, HOMOSEXUALS AND LIARS** and that

TORAH IS NOT FOR A RIGHTEOUS MAN (*1 Timothy* *1*:9–10).

– teaches that **TORAH** is WEAK AND BEGGARLY (*Galatians 4*:9).

– teaches that **A MAN CANNOT BE JUSTIFIED BY THE LAW OF MOSES** (*Acts 13*:39).

– teaches its followers to become **DEAD TO THE TORAH** (*Romans 7*:4).

– Puts a **CURSE** on any man who keeps the mitzret of Hashem (*Galatians 3*:10) says **THE TORAH IS ACCURSED** (*Galatians 3*:13).

– teaches that **NOTHING WAS MADE PERFECT BY THE TORAH OF G–D** (*Hebrews 7*:19).

EVERYDAY JEWISH SOULS ARE BEING WON TO THE HERETICAL TEACHINGS OF CHRISTIANITY. Tomorrow it could be your son or daughter who embraces the faith of a totally alien people who through the ages have ridiculed the Torah of G–D and persecuted the Jewish people.

Concerned parents and those contemplating conversion should first contact Rev Samuel Golding. Lectures on the missionary problem and how to refute missionaries will be given in universities, schools and kibbutzim. Helpful literature sent **free** at your request.

Rev Samuel Golding was born Jewish but was estranged from his roots during the holocaust. He was raised as a Christian and became a successful minister and later missionary in Paris, India and Viet Nam. After careful study of the New Testament Rabbi Golding became disillusioned with teachings of the New Testament and Christianity. He returned to Torah and Judaism. Later realising the present danger of missionary exploitation of uninformed Jews, he embarked on a campaign to make Jews aware of this danger by printing literature and lecturing on the subject on the Christian missionary threat to Judaism.

Rev Golding may be contacted at No. . . . (not Shabbat) . . . YERUHAM-ISRAEL.

Author's Footnote: Rev. Golding's Ministerial claims are extremely dubious. Enquiries at his so called places of training and ordination in Britain reveal absolutely no trace of his name or personage. Neither is there any confirmation of *any* of his many other claims to Christian experience.

APPENDIX 4

Enticement to Change of Religion

(See page 192)

Penal Code Amendment Law No. 1313 of 23.11.1977 ('Enticement to Change of Religion'). In translation the text of the law reads:

1. GIVING OF 'BONUSES' AS ENTICEMENT TO CHANGE OF RELIGION. He who gives, or promises to give money, an equivalent (of money), or other benefit in order to entice a person to change his religion, or in order to entice a person to bring about the change of another's religion, the sentence due to him is (that of) five years imprisonment, or a fine of 50,000 Israeli pounds.

2. RECEIVING OF 'BONUSES' IN EXCHANGE FOR A CHANGE OF RELIGION. He who receives, or agrees to receive money, an equivalent (of money), or a benefit in exchange for a promise to change his religion, or to bring about the change of another's religion, the sentence due to him is (that of) three years imprisonment, or a fine of 30,000 Israeli pounds.

– from United Christian Council in Israel, Newsletter, 1978, No.1.

Bibliography

BARR, Marius, *The Unholy War*, 1980.

BIVIN, David and Blizzard, Roy B., *Understanding the Difficult Words of Jesus*, 1983.

BURNETT, Ken, *Why Pray for Israel?*, 1983.

CHARIF, R & Raz, S., *Jerusalem the Eternal Bond*, 1977.

COHN, N., *Warrant for Genocide*, 1967.

CROSS, F.L., *The Oxford Dictionary of the Christian Church*, 1963.

EDERSHEIM, Alfred, *The Life and Times of Jesus the Messiah*, 1883.

EDERSHEIM, Alfred, *Sketches of Jewish Social Life*, 1876.

ELLISON, H.L., *The Mystery of Israel*, 1966.

ENCYCLOPEDIA JUDAICA, 1972.

EUSEBIUS, *The History of the Church*, 1965.

FACTS ABOUT ISRAEL, The authorised handbook to Israel 1985.

FEINBERG, Charles L., *Israel at the Center of History and Revelation*, 1980.

FISCHER, J., *The Olive Tree Connection*, 1983.

FRUCHTENBAUM, Arnold G., *Hebrew Christianity: its Theology, History and Philosophy*, 1983.

GADE, Richard E., *A Historical Survey of Anti-Semitism*, 1981.

GARTENHAUS, Jacob, *Famous Hebrew Christians*, 1979.

HISTORY UNTIL 1880, Keter Books, 1973.

HITLER, Adolph, *My Struggle*, 1933.

JOCZ, Jakob, *The Jewish People and Jesus Christ after Auschwitz*, 1981.

JOSEPHUS, F., *The Jewish War*.

LAFFIN, John, *The Israeli Mind*, 1979.

LAMBERT, Lance, *The Uniqueness of Israel*, 1980.

LAPIDE, Pinchas E., *Jesus in Israeli School Books*, *Journal of Ecumenical Studies*, Summer 1973, pp.515–531.

LAPIDE, Pinchas E., *The Last Three Popes and The Jews*, 1967.

LITTELL, Franklin H., *The Crucifixion of the Jews: the Failure of Christians to Understand the Jewish Experience*, 1975.

LLOYD GEORGE, David, *Is It Peace?*, 1923.

LOSSIN, Y., *Pillar of Fire*, 1983.

MACNAUGHTON, K.A., *The Covenants and the Promises*, 1978.

MARGOLIS, Max L., and MARX, Alexander, *A History of the Jewish People*, 1927.

MORSE, A.D., *While Six Million Died: A Chronicle of American Apathy*, 1967.

MUSSNER, Franz, *Tractate on the Jews: the Significance of Judaism for the Christian Faith*, 1984.

NEANDER, Augustus, *General History of the Christian Religion and Church*, 1871 (5 vols).

NEANDER, Augustus, *History of the Planting and Training of the Christian Church by the Apostles*, 1851 (2 vols).

PARKES, James, *The Conflict of the Church and the Synagogue*, 1969.

PRAGAI, Michael, J., *Faith and Fulfilment: Christians and the Return to the Promised Land*, 1985.

PRINCE, D., *The Last Word on the Middle East*, 1983.

PRITTIE, T & Nelson, W.H., *The Economic War Against the Jews*, 1979,

RUPP, E. Gordon, *Martin Luther and the Jews*, 1972.

SCHONFIELD, H.J., *The History of Jewish Christianity*.

SHIRER, William L., *The Rise and Fall of the Third Reich*, 1960.

SPARROW-SIMPSON, W.J., *Lectures on St Bernard of Clairvaux*, 1895.

ST JOHN, R., *Tongue of the Prophets*, 1952.

TRACHTENBERG, Joshua, *The Devil and the Jews*, 1943.

TUCHMAN, Barbara W., *Bible and Sword*, 1956.

YOUNG, Brad, *The Jewish Background to the Lord's Prayer*, 1984.